Biking, Lessons, Blessings and Beer

Across the U.S. on 14 Gears

Amos Kornfeld

Biking, Lessons, Blessings and Beer

Copyright © 2019 by Amos Kornfeld.

All rights reserved. Printed in the United States of America. No part of this book may be used or reproduced in any manner whatsoever without written permission except in the case of brief quotations embodied in critical articles or reviews.

Cover design by Jana E. Schwartz

Editing/formatting by Hannah Kornfeld

ISBN: 9780578483597

Second Edition: January 2020

CONTENTS

- INTRODUCTION 5
- VERMONT & NEW YORK 8
- PENNSYLVANIA & OHIO 47
- INDIANA & ILLINOIS 64
- IOWA 90
- NEBRASKA 110
- COLORADO 159
- WYOMING 186
- MONTANA 212
- IDAHO 251
- WASHINGTON & OREGON 260
- CALIFORNIA 293
- EPILOGUE 305

Dedication

To my parents, who even though they were at my birth, still maintain I'm adopted. I appreciate your suffering through my twisted and sometimes tortuous life's trek.

To my son, who before I embarked on a different adventure several years ago said to me, "Dad, you can't be complacent."

To my daughter, my refuge and companion at the end of my trip.

To my brother for his spirit, generosity, and sharing some of the hardest legs of the voyage. And for pestering me to write this book.

To my nephew for making it to 13 years old or I would never have biked to California this summer.

And of course, to my wife, my partner, and my love for 30-plus years. Who else would support an adventure and a person like this?

Introduction

June 8, 2017

Paradox Pond, New York

Where's the light switch? I'm looking up and down the wall next to the door. I can't find it. I scan the wall outside the stalls. I try next to the mirror, to the side of the urinals, nothing. I can't find a switch or any way to turn off the lights. It's not that bright in here and at least they're not buzzing like some fluorescent lights, I tell myself. It's 2:30 in the morning of June

BIKING, LESSONS, BLESSINGS AND BEER

8th, 2017. I'm the only person within miles; there's no one else camping at Paradox Pond State Park in the Adirondack Mountains. And I'm trying to get some sleep laying on the floor of a park bathroom, one that at least seems pretty clean, for a bathroom. My sleeping pad is keeping most of my body off the tile floor, and while I'm certainly not an eternal optimist, I know it could be worse. At least I have the shelter of the restroom.

Moments before, I'm asleep in my new-to-me bivy tent after a 100-mile day of biking. It's muggy, warm, and a breezeless night. The partial rainfly covering the tent's screen window is stifling any fresh air, so I remove it. The weather forecast says zero chance of rain. No kidding, zilch. The only reason I'm in the tent at all is because I already donated more than my fair share of blood to the mosquitoes and black flies, and they're still out in force. I'm sleeping soundly when I feel something wet on my head. In my groggy, dream-like state I'm confused.

Slowly gaining consciousness, I hear drops on the tent and realize the water on my head is rain. Maybe it will just be a few drops. I remain supine, exhausted, not minding the cool drops on my face. Then the rain starts to fall harder and now I'm getting wet. Laying still is not a viable option; my sleeping bag, gear, and I will soon be soaked. Attaching the small rainfly in the pitch-black Adirondack night in the rain is ludicrous. There's only one move—run to the bathroom about 100 yards away.

Day is done, Gone from the sun, From the lake, From the hills, From the sky; All is well...

My bike is locked to the picnic table (even though there's no one else here), and the panniers are certainly getting wet under the table, but I don't care. I grab my sleeping bag and pad and stumble to the restroom. And that's how I end up sleeping on the floor in a park bathroom, a bit wet, on my first night of what I hope will be a cross-country bicycle odyssey. What have I gotten myself into?

Vermont & New York

June 8, 2017

Norwich, Vermont to Paradox Pond, New York – 95 miles

At 6 a.m. I'm in the garage finishing the packing started the night before. It's quite cool outside, temperatures in the high 40s in spite of a brightly shining sun. I'm not going to wait for it to warm up; I want an early start having no idea how far I'll go today, my first day. I'm calling the bike "Caballo Naranjo," Orange Horse in Spanish. It's fully loaded with front and rear panniers, a tent and pad strapped atop the rear rack, and a handlebar bag in front. If ever I'm going to be ready for this journey, now is the time.

I've prepared, riding 1,000 miles during this cold and wet Vermont spring, most days bundling up and donning rain gear, neoprene booties, a hat, and mittens and biking for at least an hour and a half. On warmer days I'd ride for up to three hours. It's now 6:30 a.m. as I say goodbye to my wife, Jeannie, from the top of our driveway. It's a strange feeling, like it was before I departed on other solo trips. While this will be the longest time we've spent apart, we'll have nearly constant cell phone contact, something we didn't have when I backpacked in California or lived in South America. With emotions alternating between excitement and fear, I coast down our road.

After a gradual, 2-mile descent, I start my first climb up Beaver Meadow Road and see a familiar biker headed downhill. "This is it," I call out to Steve, who knew what I was up to. His will be the last familiar face for some time. I continue up the valley for the next 4 miles, shed a layer part way up, until I reach the height of the land, then cruise downhill into Sharon. I cycle along the White River and when I reach Royalton, I stop next to the sign marking the birthplace of Mormon founder, Joseph Smith. The temperature has warmed considerably so I strip down to a bike jersey and shorts, enjoy the warmth and sun and have my first roadside meal, a peanut butter and honey sandwich.

Back on the saddle, I pedal for a few miles, then wait behind cars so I can bike through the one lane underpass. I pedal as far to the right as I can, allowing cars to travel alongside me when a woman blasts her horn, glares at me with venom in her eyes and foists the middle finger. What the F*ck?! I don't respond; I'm too shocked. This is not a good sign for an entirely indefensible guy who counts on sharing the road with 2-ton metal beasts for the next few months. I'm less than two hours from home in bike-friendly Vermont and I'm the object of road rage? And I didn't even do anything wrong. What have I gotten myself into? This might be a long summer.

Regaining my equilibrium, I'm soon riding along Route 100 in the Green Mountain National Forest. From here on out, for the next 4,000 or so miles, every pedal will take me on a new road and sights unseen. As I come into Rochester, I spot a guy with dogs in the yard. I know my turn up to the Brandon Gap is approaching and don't want to miss it. I need water before I climb up and over the Green Mountains, so I stop at the house. This will be my first request of a stranger; a practice I know I have to master. As a blue-blooded American man, I don't ask for directions when driving a car, pre- or post-GPS. But now I've begun a cross-country bike trip, and the last thing I want to do is get lost, add extra miles, and stress.

I call out to the guy in the yard, "Helloooo...." He saunters over.

"Is there a store before I get to Route 73?" I ask. He shakes his head no.

"Can I can fill my water bottles from your spigot?"

Instead, Dave insists on taking the bottles inside and filling them from his tap. I wait in the driveway with the dogs. Handing them to me minutes later, he apologizes.

"I should have asked, do you like beer?"

Do I like beer? Do I like to bike? Dave and a friend have a fledgling brew business. He wants to know if I'll be camping and if so, will I have a place to cool a bottle of his beer?

"Sure," I say, not knowing if this is the truth. *This is a lesson that I don't need to be taught; never turn down a beer.* Little did I know that this was a sign of things to come.

Dave goes back inside his house and returns with a large, dark, label-free, brown bottle. Three hours into my trip and I'm gifted beer. How cool is this? The hell with the woman flipping me the bird. I learn my first lesson of the expedition. It pays to ask for directions.

It's now a gorgeous, Vermont summer day, 75 degrees, a light breeze, few cars, and good pavement. I make the left onto Route 73 up to the Brandon Gap. Orange construction signs line the road. On a bike, there's a bright side to road construction projects. After any cars waiting with me for the flagger to let us pass, I have the road to myself for long stretches.

I gradually climb for 9 miles with intermittent stops for more flaggers and roadwork. It's a quiet and steady ascent, not too steep, not too hot, as I ride along streams and pass occasional houses. At the summit, wow! Ahead of me are views of the Adirondack Mountains as well as a pair of bikers from Quebec, sans panniers, who are out for a day ride on a Vermont vacation. We chat a bit and I compare what we're doing. It's different in the way that day hiking is from backpacking. On a day hike you don't carry much, know where you'll sleep, it's comfortable, safe, and lacks the intensity of a backpacking trip where you carry your home on your back. I'll have my home on my bike instead of my shoulders, exposed and vulnerable. I don't know where I'll sleep and where I'll end up. This is exactly what I want.

Confident that I'm on the right path, figuratively and literally, I zoom down the western slope of the Green Mountains and pull into a general store in Brandon. Even though there's no ice cream counter, a pre-wrapped cone never tasted so good. Armed only with a state highway map, I navigate through the flatter terrain of western Vermont surrounded by orchards and farmland. I'm in the Champlain Basin headed for the Ticonderoga Ferry and stop often to check road signs and ask for directions. Riding back roads, there are no signs for the ferry, and I manage to get lost for the first time. On a 4,000-mile odyssey, being lost is relative. Nevertheless, a wrong turn finds me on a gravel road surrounded by farms, an occasional house, and still no signs for the ferry. I know I've got to be close, so when I pass a guy sitting in a screened-in porch, I stop. He lets me know that I missed my turn. I backtrack, ride a few extra miles on gravel and then reach the ferry launch in order to cross a narrow part of Lake Champlain, my most direct route to New York. Along with four motorcyclists, I wait for the return of the ferry. As a fellow motorcycle rider who's also touring on two wheels, it's easy to talk with these guys and subsequent motorcyclists. Motorcyclists and I have some things in common: we're not traveling in a metal cage, we're both on two wheels and we're touring. I like my motorcycle and considered riding it to California, but biking cross-country is a long-held dream; motorcycling is not, and I'd rather spend that many hours pedaling a bicycle.

The calm ride across the lake on the open, small, flatbed ferry ride takes 10 minutes and it's mid-afternoon when I pedal up the hill from the Lake Champlain ferry and into the town of Ticonderoga. Walking my bike in town, I spot two other bike tourers, a father and his teenage son. They started in Acadia, Maine and came through my neck of the woods to stay with family. From Colorado, they're trying to make it across the country. Impressive.

My son, Jake, is a beast and certainly wouldn't have any problem with the cycling and can rough it even better than me, but a trip this long would be hard with anyone. Now, me and my dad? And when I was a teenager to boot? Holy cow. But my father doesn't ride a bicycle and never had an interest so it's not something I dwell on. The father and son are done for the day and staying in town tonight. I wish them well, head to an air-conditioned cafe where I buy a muffin, drink ice water, and figure out what's next. I've reached my "goal" for the day; I'm in Ticonderoga, New York and out of Vermont. It feels early and I still have some energy. With over 4,000 miles to go, I don't want to stop. Since there are no places to camp in Ticonderoga, I have several choices:

1. Bike 4 miles off-route to a campground.

2. Stay in a motel in town.

3. Continue to a state park further west on the route.

4. Stealth camp—sleep in a field or woods not designated for camping.

5. Knock on a stranger's door and ask to camp on his or her property.

Options four and five are not appealing on this first day and are dismissed. Option one, biking what would end up to be 8 extra miles to the off-route, but closest campground, seems absurd. Why would I bike 8 extra miles? Since I have my camping gear and don't want to stay in a motel, biking west wins. At 4 p.m. I leave the cafe counting on another four plus hours of good light as the Siren Song serenades me.

I read an account of a cross-country bike trip in which the author described the late afternoon phenomenon of the Sirens. This gets its name from Odysseus, who along with countless sailors, was tempted by the Sirens' singing to sail to a barren island and eventual demise. On a bike trip this means being tempted to continue cycling late in the day, trying to pedal those extra miles while it's still light, even though you know that stopping makes much better sense.

I give in to the Sirens and ride on. As soon as I'm out of Ticonderoga, I'm climbing a monster hill along with plenty of cars heading home from work. Yech. I tackle the 4-mile hill as my pace slows significantly and start to feel just how tired I am. Another lesson. *Listen to those who went before.* In other words, ignore the Sirens at my own peril. The off-route campground would probably have been a wiser choice. However, at this point there's no way on God's green earth that I'm going back down the hill and east. I still have a continent to cross.

Eventually the hill ends, the road levels out, and I roll up and down the forested state highway for 14 more miles until I pull into Paradox Pond State Park. Not only is no one at the entry booth, there's nobody else in the park. I'm alone and have my choice of dozens of nearly identical campsites. I choose one, set up camp, and head to the pond for a relaxing repose. I place my bottle of beer in the water to chill and I take in the tranquility. An Adirondack pond in the forest; a beautiful spot to end my first day. I've been looking forward to that brew.

l last a few minutes. Apparently, the black flies and mosquitoes also find this to be a delightful spot and they make it impossible to enjoy the serene scene for long. The temperate water makes for no beer chilling. Still, I open the beer and drink. It's flat, warm, and not the least refreshing, even after a grueling day. I can only muster a few sips. So much for expectations. Still, I'm grateful for Dave's kindness as I head back to camp and make dinner quickly to avoid the bugs.

This is typically hardest part of the day for me: alone at night. I have little trouble pushing through the scores of miles, hills, even exhaustion. Demons at dusk are a bit more challenging. It's much harder to train my mind than my body. As much as I love the woods, being alone at night can have its creepy moments. Not tonight though. I lay in my tiny, cramped tent as darkness falls. I'm exhausted. It's been a pretty darn good first day, I'd say, and I soon fall into a deep sleep.

June 9, 2017

Paradox Pond to Blue Mountain Lake, New York – 58 miles

After last night in the restroom, I wake to a dark, damp, and cold Adirondack dawn. I don't want to cook breakfast, I want to find a warm restaurant. I munch on a Clif bar as I pack, and by 5:30 a.m.

I'm loaded and in the saddle. The early morning ride takes me up and down long hills with intermittent rain, crappy visibility, a minimal shoulder, and a ways before I'll get something hot to eat. I have the road to myself, surrounded by trees in the cool, damp shade of the great northern forest.

One of many Adirondack lakes

Less than 24 hours into my expedition, I learn another lesson. As trite as it sounds, *each day truly is a new beginning.* I can catch a few z's in a bathroom, wake up feeling like I hardly slept, a light rain falling, and still be ready to rock and roll. This doesn't mean I'm having fun; this is crappy cycling. Nevertheless, even if I'm cold, wet, and cycling through a dark morning, I am biking across the country. You know what they say, a bad day biking beats a good day at work. Every pedal brings a new sight, sound, and experience, and I have no idea what will come next. This is what I have been dreaming of. I have a goal and challenges, two things essential to my mental and physical health, and I'm on a bicycle to boot.

I'm excited to get to North Hudson where I'll get a yummy, hot meal and enjoy a warm, dry respite. After an hour and a half of wet and cold pedaling, I come to the sign announcing North Hudson. I bike through the one street in this vacant downtown and don't see anything resembling a place to get food. When I spot a guy sitting in an office, I go in and ask if there's a restaurant here. Nope, he tells me. Damn, so much for that warmth and chow. Westward Ho I go.

After cycling under Interstate 87, I see the entrance to Yogi Bear Jellystone Paradise Pines Campground. Not what I had in mind. I look at the map and see that this is where there's food and services. *I hadn't paid enough attention to learning how to read the map details.*

I'm sure there's a lesson here but not one I'm gonna learn easily.

I pedal down the driveway, under the entrance sign and to the campground store and restaurant. It's 7:30 a.m. and they don't open until 8. I don't want to wait out here for a half hour and then wait some more for them to cook my food. No one's around except a couple of maintenance guys setting up picnic tables. They say that it's fine for me to hang here. I lay my food on a table by the pool, and using a wall for wind protection, boil water for oatmeal and a cup of mocha. After all, that's why I'm carrying this stuff.

* * *

Even though I was hoping for a heartier breakfast, the oatmeal and instant coffee-hot chocolate mix warms me a bit. I have 21 more miles to Newcomb, a town denoted on the map by a star in a circle signifying all services are there: food, lodging, post office, and motel or hotel. I'm now looking at the maps more carefully. As I continue to ride in the cold drizzle, I'm even more eager for a warm respite. When I pull into and immediately out of Newcomb, population 436, the only thing I see is a food truck with a giant American flag above. That's it; no other eating options, so I backtrack to the truck.

Instead of reprinting maps each year, Adventure Cycling publishes map addenda to alert cyclists to changes. Apparently, no one told them that if Newcomb once had services, they don't any more. Food truck guy's selling hot dogs, chips, soda, and cheese on toast. Cheese on toast? Sounds like something my mom fooled us into believing was grilled cheese. Well, cheese and toast will have to do. That, and an orange soda. It's not the diner food I was hoping for but it's warm and there is no way I'm eating a hot dog; the last thing I want is to get sick. The food truck's parked in a town park/rest area with views of the High Peaks of the Adirondacks. At least the elaborate display details the peaks and their elevations that are visible on a clear day. But not today; we're socked in. That's too bad since I've backpacked the High Peaks several times, including my first ever foray 40 years ago, and it would have been awesome to see them from the seat of a bicycle.

As I eat the open-faced grilled cheese, I talk with food truck guy.

BIKING, LESSONS, BLESSINGS AND BEER

It's still gloomy and gray, he's had only one other customer since I've been here, yet he carries a genuinely grateful attitude. He tells me that this is a new endeavor for him, and he's confident that soon business will pick up with summer approaching. Good for him. His positive demeanor brightens up the dark morning. Then the rain resumes, and I head to the gazebo to finish my soda.

It's another 15 hilly miles to Long Lake, the next town which turns out to at least have a well-traveled intersection with a few stores and lodging. The sun's come out and I'm warm, dry, and happy. I lay out my wet gear and clothes on a split rail fence in front of an ice cream parlor. Unfortunately, the shop's being renovated and not yet open for the season. The Stewart's convenience store across the street will have to do. I leave my clothes to dry and bike locked to the fence, and head to the store where I buy mac and cheese, chips, and a drink.

I spend a good two hours in Long Lake. Long days are a good friend and I'm in no hurry. I've already ridden 50 miles this morning, and after yesterday's challenges, relaxing in the sun feels wonderful. After all, I've got more than two months to get to California. I gather up my dry sleeping bag and clothes and hit the road. I bike past beautiful forests and mountain lakes in a sunny breeze. This is what I'm talking about, Willis.

* * *

When I approach Blue Mountain Lake, population 130, it's late afternoon. This is another place that appears to be more of an intersection than a town, but it advertises lodging and that's what I'm after. After last night's debacle, I badly want to sleep indoors and get a good night's rest. I spot a group of young folks walking on the other side of the road carrying fishing poles. As I pass, one of them yells, "Hey Lance!" I call back, "No steroids here," assuming they're referring to Lance Armstrong. They bust up laughing. *There's no way I'll be invisible on this ride so I might as well embrace it.* Then I call the number of a motel on my map and get a recording stating they aren't yet open for the season. Damn. A sign directs me a half mile off route advertising rooms and cabins. A half mile is not 8 miles. I can handle this.

When I get to the motel and cabins, there's no one at the office, but a sign on the door offers a number to call. I do and leave a message. I try the number of the one other place in town. She's not open for the season either but thinks that the folks where I am will be able to find a place for me. I'm not so confident as it grows later. I don't see many options, so I sit in an Adirondack chair and try to enjoy the sun.

As I wait for the owners to return my call, the woman from the "not yet open inn" drives up. Weird. She assures me the owners will be here soon. The manager and his wife do show up about a half-hour later. I find out that the woman who had stopped by is a friend. Of course, there are only 130 people in town. I never quite understand why she came by. Regardless, the manager tells me not to fret, he has something for me. It's not exactly a room....

Welcome to Hotel Blue Mountain Lake, and such a lovely place…

Compared to my bivy tent, this is luxury. The manager gives me the key, his wife gives me some coffee grounds and a filter for the morning, and I bring my stuff to my temporary digs. It's similar to a motel room with a kitchenette, small bathroom, dining table, and beds. It's a heck of a lot better than a park bathroom; I'll be quite comfy.

After I unpack in my RV, I head up the hill, pass a cabin, and see a group of 20-somethings sitting and standing around a picnic table. We share greetings and then laugh when we realize who one another are. I'm "Lance" and they're the "Hey, Lance!" gang with the fishing poles. We get to talking, and before I know it, they invite me to dinner.

They are three, 20-something couples who grew up together, still live south of Buffalo, and are about as different from me as can be. We hit it off beautifully. "You're doing what?" "Biking to where?" They're flabbergasted when I describe my plans and just as amazed that I made it here in two days. "Why?" they wonder. I tell them a little about why now and my long-time love of bicycling.

The group invites me into the rented cabin where they have coolers, food, and alcohol galore. We chow on grilled chicken, chips, and veggies, drink beer and harder stuff. They are a welder, nursing assistant, sheet rocker, and students, around my own kids' ages. We're from different generations, different worlds really, and it doesn't matter a bit. *This is part of my adventure: to listen, see, and get to know my countrymen and women.*

The "Hey Lance" Gang

Later, the gang and I head out back and sit around the campfire laughing, drinking, and telling stories. I'm sure this group of 20-

somethings doesn't often party with anyone like me. Motor sports, hunting, and fishing are what they mainly do for recreation. And smoking and drinking. They have a number of coolers filled with food and drink, so I assume they're here for weeks. They tell me they're here for only three days.

A bag of chips finished, into the fire it goes. Empty cigarette packs, plastic rings from the six pack, and beer cans are tossed into the flames. It's surprising that these young folks behave with this lack of environmental consciousness, but I'm in no mood or place to give a lecture to my hosts. This is too much fun, and really, what purpose would it serve?

Being June, darkness falls late. I hang with my new friends until I have my fill of conversation and beer and become Facebook friends with Kerick. I tell them that I'll soon be in their neck of the woods near Buffalo. They're psyched and tell me to look them up if the timing works.

We bid each other warm goodnights and farewell, knowing that I'll be long gone when they wake up.

Laying in my RV, I reflect on a night full of good company and acts of generosity by people expecting nothing in return. Even though I also expanded their world and made them see new possibilities, they were the true givers. And to think, *all this was initiated by wise cracks.* A day that started with rain, hunger, and cold, ends by a warm fire, full of food and beer, in the company of new friends, and a bed in an RV.

June 10, 2017
Blue Mountain Lake to Redfield, New York – 101 miles

As I bike the Adirondacks this morning, it's a whole different world. The sun is shining, I'm rested, and my surroundings of lakes, rivers, and hills are stunning. My first stop of the day is the quaint village of Old Forge. At a bike shop I ask if they have a bolt for my shoe cleat as I lost one. They don't, but I'm okay riding the way it is. The shop is busy for being this early in the morning on account of a local bike race, hence the number of cars carrying bikes that pass me.

I mosey down the sidewalk and stop at a bakery where I dine on a delicious homemade donut, order coffee, and fill my water bottles. I spit out the coffee; it's salty. Have you ever drunk salty coffee? Don't. One of the nastiest beverages I've tried. Thankfully a kind waitress at the restaurant across the street fills my bottles with salt-free ice water.

Ten miles later I reach McKeever and am routed off the state highway onto meandering Moose River Road, speed limit 35. I ride in the shade paralleling a roaring mountain river with gentle rolling hills, magnificent cycling. For the most part, I have the road to myself

BIKING, LESSONS, BLESSINGS AND BEER

and eventually the woods and river views are replaced by houses and yards, most simple, unoccupied, and many dilapidated.

As a comfortably warm morning starts to get steamy, I'm in a good mood, the effects from the night before lingering along with mighty fine biking. My bike holds two water bottles, and at this point I haven't thought to use my Camelback insulated water pouch that I can wear on my back. My water bottles are empty, so when I see a woman outside her home down a long driveway, I park my bike against the mailbox.

"Good morning!" I holler. "Do you have any water?" She doesn't respond and instead goes inside. Hmmm. I'm not sure what she's up to so I wait at the bottom of the driveway. A few minutes later she returns with a few small bottles of water in her hand. I walk up the drive to meet her. She's small, looks to be about 70, and as she hands the bottles to me says, "Stay here." I take it to mean that she doesn't want me to come any closer to her house. I must look more threatening than I thought. Then she says, "My husband wants to give you something." Okay....

While I wait for her to return, I down one of the bottles of cold water. Minutes later she comes back with granola bars and more water. She seems to be warming up and tells me her husband is disabled; that's why he's inside and why she told me to wait. I let her know I'm appreciative of the cold water and treats.

I'm back riding on the byways of New York, and soon I'm not sure if I'm going the right way. I think I'm supposed to make a left, but there's no road signs at the intersection. The map directions tell you when and at what mile (or tenth of a mile) to turn, but that assumes you have not deviated from the route and are paying careful attention to the odometer. I'm doing neither. Since there's no one around this rural stretch, after about a mile I decide to turn around. I stop when I get back at the intersection. I figure that this has got to be my turn, but I have no way of knowing. I'm riding through extremely rural New York on a route that seems to avoid every town. I did make the right turn, as I'm soon on a named road that matches the directions. In an hour I'm thirsty and out of water, again.

I see "Yard Sale" signs in front of a modest house and slow down. There's a guy out back who I assume is the homeowner. I park my bike and call out, "Hellooo!" The man approaches and when I ask for water, he and his wife invite me to sit at their patio table. He goes inside and returns with ice water, a banana, and Chex mix. The three of us sit and chat. I try to be discreet while I eat everything they've laid out. They are kind, tell me they love where they live, their only complaint being their daily commute to Utica, an hour each way. More acts of kindness still close to home and very heartening. I had no idea that this is what I'd experience.

With temperatures now in the mid-80s, I'm fading. The 10 miles to Booneville takes longer than I hoped. Booneville, population 2,072, is the biggest town since Ticonderoga, and I plan to take a long rest and evaluate my next move. I'm making good progress and am still not sure what I'm capable of.

As great as they are, the Adventure Cycling maps only show the bike route and not the surrounding areas. A state map would sure be handy for some perspective. I know I'm getting closer to my friend Annie who lives a little ways off the route. As I approach town, I stop at the Booneville Black River Canal Museum. It'a an historic building, homey and full of artifacts commemorating the importance of this canal that connects to the Erie Canal, but I'm on a mission: ice cream. The best ice cream is 2 miles away, off route, the woman working here tells me. "Anything in town?" I ask. She tells me that there's one other shop in town, and since I am so friggin' hot, I am not going extra miles, even for better ice cream. I figure any ice cream will do. Silly me.

I get to town and stop at the Booneville Library to look over maps and find a route to Annie's. When I ask the librarian for a map or gazetteer, she's surprised. She can't remember the last time someone asked to look at a map. We climb the stairs and find a New York Gazetteer buried in the stacks. I peruse the atlas and call Annie. I tell her that I think I'll make it to her home tomorrow.

Directly behind the library is a restaurant with an ice cream window, the other ice cream in town. I don't even have to put on my shoes to walk over. While any ice cream is a treat in this heat, the ice cream is good, not great. I hope I learn another lesson. *When someone recommends great ice cream, ride the extra miles.*

It's now the middle of the afternoon and with the tasty ice cream a memory, I have two choices. One is to keep riding, the other is to stay here. Since I have zero desire to spend six daylight hours in Booneville, here we go again. I've biked 60 miles so far today. Before starting the trip, I figured if I average 80 miles a day, I'll make it to California with time to take a few days off. Any days that I ride more miles will give me flexibility if weather or other problems arise. Now the Sirens are calling once more, tempting me. Didn't I learn that lesson? Apparently not because off I go. I have no idea what the terrain or wind portend, but I do know that the upcoming towns are small and spread out. In moments I'm back in the boonies outside Booneville, of course. The westerly wind picks up and 8 long miles later I reach the junction at West Leyden. A candy bar and the soda fountain from the convenience store temporarily revive me. I have another 25 miles to Redfield, the next town with lodging since I'm not confident about staying dry in the bivy tent and the skeeters make sleeping without a tent ludicrous. If I ride 12 miles per hour, I can be there in two hours. I'm committed; there's nothing else before Redfield and going back is not an option. I am not having fun.

BIKING, LESSONS, BLESSINGS AND BEER

Other than a few souped up cars zooming past me, I'm riding alone through dilapidated fields and homes. These folks look like they're either being left behind by the 21st century or they chose to stay back. This is rural, poor New York, a far cry from downstate where I grew up. I bike past many more run-down and abandoned farms, houses, and shacks than I do tidy homes. The fields are overgrown and littered with rusted machines, mile after mile, one endless Tobacco Road.

Whipped, I finally cross the Salmon River and Reservoir and enter the town limits of Redfield. I just completed a century ride through heat, wind, and on a loaded bike. I'm beat but I'm okay. On my right is the Crossroads Inn and Cabins. Overlooking the reservoir and river, it looks beautiful, and upscale. Not for me, too ritzy, especially since I only plan to sleep and head out the next morning. I hope there are other places to stay. If not, will I splurge for a cabin, spend another night sweating in the bivy, or expose myself to the blood sucking and buzzing black flies and mosquitoes? I pedal into town, which of course consists of only an intersection, but there's also a bar, Redfield Square. I lock my bike outside and head in. It's dark, quiet, rustic, like something out of the '70s. I ask a guy seated at the bar if there's any place to stay in town. He directs me to a place that rents rooms down the road. I thank him and let him know that I'll be back.

About a mile down the road's a small motel with a restaurant and store. I think I'm the only one staying here. The room and the setting are sterile, but the air conditioning feels amazing. After a well-deserved and much-needed shower, I bike back up the road to the bar.

Redfield Square is now hopping. Most of the town must be here; kids, teens, and adults are milling about outside in the warm summer evening. I park my bike among the four-wheelers, pick-ups, and side-by-side utility vehicles and lock it to a post. I feel odd locking my bike in this out-of-the-way neighborhood locale where everybody knows one another, but I know I should; it takes only seconds to steal a bike.

When I was 12 years old, I had a green Schwinn Varsity 10 speed, my first touring bike. The Schwinn meant fun, speed, and freedom. I rode that bike everywhere. One evening I biked down the road to the drugstore to get a candy bar. I left the bike out front knowing I'd just be a minute. When I came out my beloved bike was gone. I looked all around the shopping centers. No green Varsity. It vanished and I was in shock. I ran home, told my father, we got in his car and drove for hours all around the neighborhoods searching for my bike. No luck. I felt violated. For years, I was on the lookout for that bike, even after I had gotten a new one. From that day on, I've always locked my bike.

* * *

BIKING, LESSONS, BLESSINGS AND BEER

In the bar I take a stool next to John, the guy who earlier told me about the nearby motel. I picked the right seat and the right guy. He's friendly from the get-go, has a good sense of humor, likes to talk, and if he isn't the actual mayor of Redfield, he should be. Seems like John knows everyone, all 500 of the town's residents, including the summer ones. As people come in, they banter with him, especially about the day's earlier events. I listen and eventually chime in.

"Let me get this right. It's a beautiful, sunny, 80-degree day and you guys are snowmobiling?"

"Skimming on the lake," John corrects me. I may have heard of this sport, but I know I've got a puzzled expression.

"This weekend's the Spring Classic Watercross," adds another guy. That would be something to see.

I ask, "What happens if you sink?"

"If you hit the water at the right speed, keep the throttle open, you can skim."

"And the guy you were laughing about whose sled sank?"

"All he's gotta do is clean the water out of the carburetor, exhaust, and spark plugs, replace the fuel, and he's good to go."

Sitting at a bar and drinking light beer with the locals in Redfield, New York. I remember the Rock Cut, the bar that my grandparents owned in Peekskill, New York when I was a kid. Both bars are both from a similar era. My Poppa Jack and Nannie Annie ran the Rock

Cut and my dad, uncles, and aunt helped out when they were younger. My grandfather was the most chill guy I knew, but that wasn't always the case. My dad said there were nights when the bar looked like the Wild West with tables flying and chairs broken. My pops didn't take anyone's b.s. One time, my father told me, a guy rode in on his motorcycle. Into the bar. Poppa Jack picked up the bike and threw it and the guy outside. He was a bull. But I only remember that he and my grandmother were incredibly generous and there were always strangers and visitors over for dinner.

I have another question for John.

"Why are all these folks drinking light beer?"

Although not as hefty as some of the other, John's a big guy too. Deadpanned, he tells me, "People want to watch their weight." I have to bite my lip. I'm not sure if he's joking.

I eat a lousy burger, chips, and drink a few light beers, but it's the company that makes this evening great. A couple of transplants from Pennsylvania stand with us and tell me about the area and how much snow they get in the winter. Only 20 miles from Lake Ontario, last winter they received a mighty generous gift of 29 feet of snow. That's 348 inches, making this the snowiest place in the Great Lakes region. No wonder this is a mecca for snowmobiling. What I wouldn't give to ski and snowshoe in that kind of snow. Shoveling would be another story.

BIKING, LESSONS, BLESSINGS AND BEER

As darkness falls, it feels like time to head to the motel. It's sinking in that it's not just new sights and places that this journey will bring, it's the people. I'm not a guy who typically dines or goes to bars alone, yet here I am, a fairly progressive Vermonter laughing and hanging out in a redneck bar.

June 11, 2017

Redfield to Lake Canandaigua, New York – 81 miles

As usual, I wake up at dawn, my favorite time to ride. Roads are at their quietest, I feel rested, and the temperatures are at their most comfortable. Believing that my motel is off the Adventure Cycling route, I backtrack to the empty bar and look for the right road. I'm baffled. There aren't road signs; that would be too easy. I bike out and back on the main road until I get to the Salmon Reservoir where I came in yesterday. Then I try a side road. Nope. At least once a day I get lost, just not usually first thing in the morning. I'm not upset; it isn't like I have a deadline or appointment ahead. At 6 a.m. on a Sunday morning, there aren't a lot of folks around to ask directions. I am perplexed. After 15 minutes pedaling in and around Redfield, I'm back at the motel. Checking my map again, it appears that the motel actually is on the route. Having demonstrated my map reading aptitude once again, I think, "This cross-country odyssey may be even longer than I anticipated."

I head due west and soon can catch glimpses of Lake Ontario in the distance. The riding is unremarkable. I check out a breakfast place but don't like the vibe, so go to a convenience store for a snack and a drink and keep going. By the time I get to Sodus Point, it's afternoon; probably as good a place as any to head south off-route to Annie's. I call to get directions and Annie tells me that her brother, Jared, and his girlfriend will soon be in the general vicinity of Sodus Point. Since he lives next to Annie, they're going to swing by and pick me up. Sweet. I unpack my bike, take off the wheels, panniers, and pump so that it's ready load into Jared's car when he arrives an hour later.

Overlooking Lake Canandaigua with Annie

BIKING, LESSONS, BLESSINGS AND BEER

It's good to chat with Jared, who I've only heard about, until he drops me at Annie's, a stunning spot overlooking Lake Canandaigua.

A few hours later, I'm eating a yummy home-cooked dinner with Annie and her mom, a treat any time but especially so after four days of being with strangers or alone. Annie is stoked about my trip, and I'm again made aware of how much I am spreading good tidings and not only taking. Since I'm out of the mountains and summer's heating up, it's an excellent time to rid myself of extra baggage. Annie's headed to Vermont in a few weeks, so I leave her with my two books, a jacket, and some other clothes that I don't think I need. *Doesn't this usually seem to be the case? We carry a lot more baggage than we need.*

June 12, 2017
Lake Candandaigua to Lockport, New York – 90 miles

After a delightful visit with Annie, I'm ready to roll this morning. At other times in my life I may have departed with less enthusiasm, relishing the familiarity and security. Not now. Westward Ho, baby. Annie insists on dropping me off on her way to work. She doesn't want me biking the narrow roads near her home, and while I protest, I acquiesce to my generous host.

From where Annie leaves me, it's several miles to Macedon, the

Erie Canal, and its parallel towpath. This "detour" with motorized assists from Annie and her brother form a "V," so I am not the beneficiary of any "free" miles. All the better.

I bike through Palmyra where I encounter a gigantic temple seemingly in the middle of nowhere. What the …? Turns out that the temple sits on the land where Joseph Smith discovered the Book of Mormon on the Hill Cumora. It's like I'm on a Mormon pilgrimage; on my first day I rode past Joseph Smith's birthplace and now this.

A few miles later I'm riding along the banks of the famed Erie canal which I only know from the song:

Low bridge, everybody down,

Low bridge for we're coming to a town.

And you'll always know your neighbor,

And you'll always know your pal

If you've ever navigated on the Erie Canal.

It doesn't look like such a big deal now. Today, the Erie Canal is only used for recreation because it's too narrow and shallow for the behemoths that are today's ships. Started in 1817, it took 8 years to complete the 363-mile-long, 4-feet-deep, and 40-feet-wide canal that was later expanded to 7 feet deep and 70 feet wide. In 1825, the stagecoach from Albany to Buffalo took two weeks; the canal sped things up to a 5-day jaunt, and I can do it even faster pedaling on two wheels.

BIKING, LESSONS, BLESSINGS AND BEER

The path is mostly deserted except when I approach a town where people are walking, cycling, jogging, and relaxing. Geese are another story. There are frequent gaggles of geese on all sides that scatter as I approach. Some waddle towards the canal, others meander off to the grass, some run, others mosey off. They always get off the path. At noon, I come to a flock of what must be 100 adults and goslings on the trail. They scatter; most go a good distance away and a few shuffle just off the path. I split the flock as a few of the big birds squawk at me. Then one charges, hissing and flapping his wings. He's on me, thrashing and hissing and then he nips my leg! Damn; bitten by a wild goose. I know I'll eventually ride through Yellowstone and grizzly country, but geese most definitely are not on my list of animal predators to be wary of. For the rest of my time on the towpath, I slow down when I see geese, yell, and give them time to move. It works. I'm not attacked again.

Riding the canal this morning is peaceful and a breeze, or I should say, no breeze. Flat with only a gentle wind, I cruise. But by mid-afternoon, I'm riding into a stiff headwind and it is beginning to suck my energy and my mood. I take breaks at almost every town, about 10 miles apart, and climb a bridge spanning the canal to get a better view of this flat landscape. The only true break in the monotony is a half-hour detour through construction in Rochester where I am led off the path along busy roads and get confused in a city park. By the end of the afternoon on the canal I've had more than enough, especially of the wind. "Oh yeah," a local tells me, "the towpath's a wind tunnel." I didn't expect this; another of the shortfalls of limited trip planning.

"Low bridge, ev'rybody down," 120 miles alongside the Erie Canal

By evening, I reach Lockport and I'm done with the canal, thank goodness. I find a motel a few miles away, walk to a Mexican restaurant and dine while talking on the phone with Jeannie. Until I pick up my tent, hopefully a few days from now in Cleveland, I'm resigned to staying in motels. Some folks like motels with their beds and showers. Not me. I find them isolating and confining and much prefer camping. It's easier to meet and hang out with people where you're not walled off and locked away in your own cubicle.

BIKING, LESSONS, BLESSINGS AND BEER

June 13, 2017

Lockport to Hamburg, New York – 60 miles

Scott Goodman was a badass long before I knew that term. In large part, I attribute this whole cockamamie endeavor to him. It began around 1976. Scott lived in the townhouse building next door to ours, was 5 years older than me, too old to play basketball, stickball, and kick the can with us, but we knew one another. There were two things I remember about Scott: The first was that he threw a serious frisbee and won competitions. One time, he and I walked up to the high school to throw. As we got near the school, a couple of my peers started yelling anti-semitic words at us from their front porch. I would have ignored it, but not Scott. He walked right up to them. I couldn't hear what he said, but they didn't utter another word.

The second was that Scott knew bikes; he was the bike whisperer to a suburban kid like me. He helped me learn to change a flat tire and he had told me that he had ridden cross-country, I believe twice. I remember thinking how cool that was, riding your bicycle across the U.S. In 1976, who did that?

It wasn't as though biking across the U. S. of A. was something I'd always wanted to do. As much as I loved biking as a kid, going across the whole country seemed absurd. Besides, what was there to see between the east and west coasts? And how would you get across the western mountains? That was my thinking for about 40 years, until last year, when I first entertained this idea. I love biking, I love challenges, I crave goals and a degree of structure, I have work that allowed me to do it, and I have to go to California. Voilà.

That's part of the explanation why I'll be passing Niagara Falls today. My nephew has a bar mitzvah on August 19th in California, and I had told myself that if I were going to California for another family event, I am not going by plane.

Adventure Cycling's route has me going through Canada, likely to avoid Buffalo, and maybe because they think Niagara Falls is worth the detour. I'm glad to avoid as much urban riding as I can for so many reasons. City biking with its plethora of cars, few if any shoulders, and the need to to constantly focus on the road conditions, potholes, street signs, buses, cars, delivery trucks, car doors, and people is far from enjoyable. Also, a loaded bike is not a nimble machine and I might as well be sporting a flashing neon "tourist" sign. As if these aren't enough reasons to make me dislike urban cycling, I feel much more vulnerable in the in the city than country. So, I choose the roundabout route through the land of the mounties, maple leafs, and Molson toward Niagara Falls.

The cycling is fine on this gray day. I enjoy a breakfast sandwich

BIKING, LESSONS, BLESSINGS AND BEER

on the porch of a small, country store, I pass through my first Native American Reservation and see signs for cheap gas and cigarettes, and then I get to the Canadian border. The signs are much harder to follow for bikes than cars, but after getting redirected by the border agent, I am cycling in Canada. All is well as I pass a botanical garden, an adventure park, a butterfly garden, a zoo, and then I reach the casinos and hotels. Eesh. Then come the Falls. I walk my bike through the crowds of tourists and know I'd feel out of place on a tour bus or in a car and feel even more so on a loaded bike. Niagara Falls may have been majestic before development wrecked the area, but traffic and commercialism make me want to move on. I take photos and a short rest and head back towards the U.S.

As I cycle along the Niagara River towards the New York border, I hear an odd noise coming from the back of my bike, a clicking sound, and even though I look when I cycle and check it out when I stop, I can't figure out what's causing it. My first mechanical issue. Luckily, I soon come to a bike shop and stop in. Also, my crotch is sore, and I wonder if it's worth buying some of that fancy chamois cream.

Fully loaded on the Canadian side of the falls.

    The shop's empty except for the owner and when I tell him my problem, he tells me to take my panniers off, put my bike in the stand and pedal. With the panniers on, I couldn't see the end of the brake cable hitting the wheel at regular intervals. Simple. Bike mechanic man solves it by bending the cable. I ask him about the chamois cream. He doesn't think it's worth the money. The vaseline I'm using works just as well if I don't mind it being a bit messier. He also suggests that I stand up on the pedals frequently to let my parts know they are alive. Ha! I thank bike mechanic man and continue south. I follow his advice, and while I occasionally need vaseline, I feel better and regularly stand on the pedals.

    Following the directions for bikers, I reach a building at the U.S.-Canadian border where a sign on the door tells me to ring a bell. I do and wait a few minutes for the border guard. In the meantime, I try

BIKING, LESSONS, BLESSINGS AND BEER

to psyche myself up to navigate through part of Buffalo. It's incredible that 12 hours after having started biking this morning, I'm still motoring along with plenty of daylight ahead, biked in and out of Canada, and still don't know where I'm headed tonight or beyond.

When I left my home a few days ago, I had no idea of what I was getting into. Truly. As I approach my first city, this is apparent; if not to observers, then to me. Up until now, I've been riding through countryside, the mountains, and small towns, all well within my comfort zone. Sure, I bike a lot, but not for distance and not touring. I've done a few century rides in my valley, a bike tour on Cape Cod when I was 15, and a bike trip with Jeannie in Washington state almost 30 years ago. I've traveled a fair amount alone and with others, and have a good bike, a credit card, and more than adequate equipment. I'm also headstrong and persistent and I read others' accounts of biking cross-country. But riding across the country, day after day, alone? Much to learn has this no-so-young padawan. No matter how much training, planning, and researching I did or didn't do, I'll never know what it will be like until I do it. So other than being in shape, taking what I thought was the right gear, and carrying maps, I didn't plan too much. I have a combination of enough confidence, bravado, and ignorance to I hope I'll figure it out.

Border guard opens the gate for me to pass through and I follow the route through Buffalo during rush hour, stopping when I spot a large outdoor pavilion. It seems like a good time for a break. I buy a drink and withdraw money from an ATM. There are folks hanging out in the pavilion on big comfy chairs and at tables, and even though I'm obviously bike touring, people are doing their own things, and no one approaches or converses with me. This reinforces my disdain for city travel. I chill for a bit and soon after resuming my ride, I'm lost on an unfriendly, shoulder-less, four-lane avenue leading to the interstate. So different from navigating on country roads. Riding to the right on busy roads, watching for all sorts of vehicles, traffic lights, and cars coming and going, it's hard to attend to directions and street signs. I turn around and am back on route.

Eventually I'm out of the city and in suburban Orchard Park. I stop at a Subway to fill my water bottles, talk with a few folks, and decide to push on as evening approaches. I make it to Hamburg, a small city near Orchard Park where I see a great looking ice cream shop with picnic tables, families playing, and kids in baseball uniforms. I haven't had dinner, but I'm an adult. I can eat ice cream whenever I want. However, it's starting to get dark and first I want to find a place to stay. I pedal on, planning to return for the ice cream. After several miles of semi-urban crappy riding, I cross I-90 and find a Motel 6. Yep, it's as cheap in all the ways you've heard, but I just want to get sleep and not bed bugs, another predator absent from my list.

BIKING, LESSONS, BLESSINGS AND BEER

I didn't plan on being a credit card biker and staying in motels. After all, I am hauling my camping gear. Between my lack of a tent and being in urban areas, I'm starting to act like one. Credit card biking and camping are just two of the the several ways I know of how folks bike across the country. Many join a catered group where essentially, you're only responsible for pedaling, shifting, and steering. Your gear is in a van, navigation is left to a paid leader, and meals are eaten at restaurants or prepared for you.

By the time I check into my motel room, much less inviting than my RV mind you, there's no way I'm heading several miles back on that crappy road for ice cream. It would also mean biking back in the dark. There's a family in the pool and we get to talking. The mom's a competitive triathlete and the dad's a biker, retired from the military and has time to support her. We talk for a while until I'm too hungry. My dining consolation prize is my first Tim Hortons. No ice cream, but surprisingly tasty chili and cornbread, even if I may not be the best food critic after over 100 miles of biking, two border crossings and lots of urban navigation, *and still I have not yet learned the lesson about stopping for great ice cream.*

Pennsylvania & Ohio

June 14, 2017

Hamburg, New York to Conneaut, Ohio – 110 miles

I wake without bed bugs, and after packing, I stop in the Motel 6 office to see what breakfast offerings they have. None. There's only lousy coffee with non-dairy, powdered cream, better than nothing. Maybe. It's on to my first-ever Walmart Supercenter to purchase sunscreen and groceries. Living the dream. A few miles later, off in the distance, I can make out Lake Erie. I will parallel the southern shore of this Great Lake for the next 100 miles. I stop at Lake Erie State Park to enjoy the beach for a bit, and while there, chat with some rangers. Nearly 10,000 square miles in area, Lake

BIKING, LESSONS, BLESSINGS AND BEER

Erie's supposed to be the warmest of the Great Lakes. My feet manage to test the waters on this cool morning. Still, it is a great lake. Minus the waves and salt water, it looks more like an ocean: water as far as I can see and no distant shore.

I ride along the Great Lake for the rest of the day, most of the time still in New York and I can't believe it. Even though I'm a native New Yorker, I had no idea that New York's this huge, especially its width. Today is my seventh day cycling west, and I have spent some or all of each day pedaling though the Empire State. I don't think there will be another state that I'll pedal through for so long with the possible exception of California, a long way off.

Lake Erie: no saltwater and no sharks

As I roll through Lake City, a bicyclist coming from the other way does a U-turn to meet me. He asks where I'm headed. He's impressed and tells me that he's riding from Minnesota to Virginia as part of a fundraising effort for some cause with a pink ribbon. A little while earlier I saw a car announcing this, and I ask him if he's part of a group. "No, that's my wife in the car. She drives and we meet up throughout the day." Add this to the list of ways to bike cross-country. Ride your own ride. I wish him well and he makes his second U-turn.

* * *

I reach Erie, Pennsylvania around rush hour, something about cities and rush hours it seems. I take a cool break at the library, and while there's a park here that offers camping, I've heard bad things about Erie, so I continue west. With only 80 stress-free miles behind me, of course I cycle on. Friggin' Sirens. After 90 miles, I'm beat and there's nowhere around to sleep. I come to an ice cream shop in what once was a bank, complete with a drive-through window. I lean my bike against a picnic table, nixing the drive-through idea. The ice cream is okay, and I motor on, hoping to find a place to sleep soon.

I'm beginning to understand a key difference between traveling by bike and by car. *When biking, it's the traveling itself, the movement, the process, the flow. The voyage is as much or more than the destination.* I'm getting there. I'm still focused on Montana and California but I'm settling into the groove, although not so much when I'm spent.

By the time I reach Conneaut, Ohio, it's well into the evening.

BIKING, LESSONS, BLESSINGS AND BEER

I've cycled in three different states today and I've had enough. A guy on the street tells me there's a place to stay near the water. I'm in no mood for exploring, so I follow his advice and directions to the Lakefront Inn. The office is locked. Great. There's a sign on the door and a number to call. Not again. It's getting darker and I have no idea if there are available rooms, but it's not as if I have appealing choices. I call, leave a message, and this time I get a call back almost immediately. She has a room! The manager's across the way at what looks like a swanky venue, the Conneaut Boat Club, and will be here in a minute. Manager woman comes over, seeming slightly tipsy, registers me, and shows me to my room. I'm hungry for dinner and ask if I can join her at the club, mostly joking. "No," she says, "members only."

I don't want to ride around looking for a place to eat, so I decide to treat myself to the closest place around, just down the hill from the inn and on the water, the Breakwall BBQ. Soulful music's playing as I sit outside overlooking the bay, the setting sun, and thoroughly enjoy a local beer, ribs, cornbread, and great music.

It's almost closing time and not busy, so my waitress spends a lot of time at my table. She's the mother of a few elementary students and works as a paraprofessional in two schools. She dreams of being a teacher, and I tell her that I think she has the chops. Hopefully, I encouraged her to follow her passion. I realize she's the first person I connected with all day.

June 15, 2017
Conneaut to Solon, Ohio – 74 miles

"Welcome to Ashtabula, Home of Urban Meyers." An hour and a half after leaving Conneaut, this is the sign that announces I'm entering Ashtabula. For those of you who don't know, Urban is the football coach of the "Oh How I Hate Ohio State" Buckeyes, arch nemesis of our beloved Michigan Wolverines and kicker of our asses 15 of the last 16 years. We've never beaten him. In spite of this trivia, Conneaut is a picturesque small city on Lake Erie at the mouth of Conneaut Creek. I have real coffee in a cafe with a neat vibe and more good music. I chat with the barista and chill by the water for a while. Summertime and the livin' is easy.

Next, I'm in Geneva-on-the-Lake, a summer tourist town but almost deserted on this June morning that has turned cooler and drizzly. I consider waiting out the rain, but it's light, so I power on. I'm choosing my own route for the first time since Ticonderoga, heading to Solon, Ohio where I hope to be united with a tent and my cousin, Lori. I'm psyched.

On the way, I stop in Chardon, only slightly off-route, and stop in the tourist bureau on the common to get a map. But they have nothing of use. What happened to good ole paper maps? Walking around the farmers market on the green, I chat with vendors, folks from environmental organizations, and a cheesemaker. Mr. Cheesemaker tells me that he once took a long-distance bike ride when he was poor as a church mouse. People were kind to him, and he insists on giving me a block of cheese. I oblige, of course, and am the recipient of a delicious pound of his artisan cheese.

Otherwise, it's uneventful riding. More cars and fewer shoulders, a downside of not being on an Adventure Cycling route, which intentionally takes you off the high-density roads when feasible. The end of the day has me cycling on beautiful, hilly, shoulder-less, country roads with well-maintained stone walls, stunning stone buildings, and horses. It reminds me of Landenberg, Pennsylvania, Jeannie's hometown. Who knew the suburbs of Cleveland are steeped in beautiful countryside? After another end-of-the-day monster hill, I arrive at Susie's house, my sister-in-law's cousin. She's not here, but she did tell me how to get in and to make myself at home. I take off the wheels and panniers, hose down my bike, take a refreshing shower, and munch. And munch some more. There's a veritable smorgasbord of yummy goods in two fridges and cupboards. When Susie, arrives I find her warm and gracious, and we chat until Lori arrives. Lori and I drive the few hours to her home in Columbus, catching up, and I am super excited for a respite with family.

June 16, 2017

Bexley and Columbus, Ohio

Lori and I grew up 1 year and 20 miles apart, and as a teen I biked to her house a few times, an expedition for a youngster. Not even that much cycling on the agenda today. I am taking, in hiking vernacular, "a zero day." Today I will not get on my bicycle. Instead, my cousin, her son Eli, and I tour Ohio State University, including the famed football stadium, the "Horseshoe."

With Cousin Lori in Hell

We drive to North Market, I continue to eat well, and we chill at their house. It's great to feel at home and enjoy family. That

BIKING, LESSONS, BLESSINGS AND BEER

evening Lori, her husband Brian, Eli, and I enjoy a spectacular Italian dinner at a local restaurant. I decide here and now that I'll take days off more often. I feel mentally and physically rejuvenated and this also serves to temper my need for more miles. I do have a tendency to rush.

I think there's something to the Torah's precept, *"On six days work may be done, but on the seventh day you shall have a Sabbath of complete rest."*

Upon leaving Annie, and now, Lori, it feels like my adventure is truly beginning. I've driven from Vermont to Ohio in 12 hours on the interstates, one day in a car. And even though I've been cycling for 9 days, it still feels like I'm not too far from home. But this is the last of the familiar until I reach my son in Montana, thousands of miles west. The foray enters a new phase.

June 17, 2017

Bexley to Middlepoint, Ohio – 103 miles

The morning starts north of Columbus because my cousin won't have me ride through Columbus, even on a Saturday morning. She's been an incredible host, so I oblige, and she drops me in Dublin. Since Columbus is south of my route, this results in my second Ohio "V" detour and another net gain of zero "free" miles. Lori and I share a grateful goodbye and I promise to keep her posted on my progress.

Twenty miles after leaving Lori, I reach Marysfield and pass little league baseball. I spent many hours playing and coaching little league, and I'm excited to check out the scene, meet some folks, the whole midwest, baseball, and apple pie Americana. I go to the town building to use the restroom when I'm confronted by a snarling woman. "This building is reserved for a baby shower," she barks, and I am unceremoniously shown the door. So much for my being special. I head to the bleachers, watch warm-ups, am not approached by anyone, and actually feel out of place. So much for my expectations; onwards towards Lima. There's nothing special about Lima, just an easy target to aim for on my way to Indiana.

Although I used Google Maps to get to Susie's in Solon, this is the first time I'm going into the unknown with no plan until I reach the Adventure Cycling route in Indiana. I can take any road, go anywhere. There's no one and no thing telling me I can't. It's a big country and I have so many choices.

This part of Ohio is shadeless farmland and it's getting hot. I bike through sleepy Raymond with its 257 people who are probably inside their cool houses, and I pass a few folks seated on a porch. I give a wave and as I pass, I think I hear them call me. I stop and backtrack. The boombox radio is blasting Aerosmith and it's hard to hear them.

BIKING, LESSONS, BLESSINGS AND BEER

They're motioning for me to join them. Why not? I'm getting better at saying yes. I introduce myself, shake hands, and one of the trio heads inside and returns with a couple of bottles of water.

Refreshments in Raymond

I stand with the threesome and drink a bottle of refreshingly cold water. They offer a seat, but being in the saddle for so long, I remain standing. In addition to, or instead of water, the guy with the cup has clearly drank quite a bit of something stronger than water. He's happily inebriated and I can't understand half of what he says due to the alcohol, a speech impediment, or something else. Two Sheets to the Wind is a gracious host and offers me rum. I thank him but decline, telling them I still have miles to go. There isn't much to do in Raymond, they tell me, so they must find me as entertaining as I find them. Again, I have a good time with folks that I most certainly would not have, had I not been on two wheels. They make me feel I could stay as long as I want.

Restored, I pedal on. After another hot, long, open stretch, I come to scattered houses with big trees in front. I slow down to scope out a place to rest in the shade. I see grass and trees just beyond a house. As I dismount, a couple of guys head to a truck in the driveway. One's getting in, the other, apparently the homeowner, sees me and calls out, "I'm about to let my dogs out. You might want to get moving." Really dude? I haven't had a problem with dogs yet and don't want to start now, especially from a stand still. Seems like he is giving me a head start. Although I may be on his property, I'm just off the road and past his house, clearly not bothering anyone. I'm not in any position to argue and don't want to engage this guy, so I heed his warning and pedal off shaking my head. A rare arse. From a welcome of cold water and rum to a threat, all within the hour.

In a while I come to a drive-through beverage establishment. I ought to bike through the tunnel. That would be cool, but not knowing what I want as well as wanting a break, I park and walk in. The owner asks me what I'd like. "Can I walk back and see what you have?"

I can't. He tells me that once a person walked back there and fell, causing an insurance kerfuffle and since then people aren't allowed out of their vehicles. I buy a too-sweet iced tea and potato chips. I'm loving chips on this ride, must be the salt. As I munch and drink, I talk with the guy. What's life like here? Who is he? What makes him tick? I'm genuinely curious and have the time to find out. Sports memorabilia hang on the wall, including a Yankees banner and photos, a great opening for me.

"Why the Yankees?" I ask.

"My father's a big fan." The proprietor is intelligent and articulate. Growing up here on a farm with eight siblings, he knows Lima. He tells me times are harder now, fewer manufacturing and farming opportunities. I'm in the heart of the Rust Belt; the city has lost about a quarter of its population since the seventies and home values are near the bottom of the state, as is the household income. When homes sell for $27,000 each, it's obvious that real estate doesn't seem to be in much demand. Everyone in his family's still around except his parents who have gone south. He's itching to get out, but with kids still at home and his wife's parents here, it will be several years until he can do it.

Leaving the beverage mart in the mid-afternoon, I think about the liberating feeling I have most mornings not knowing where I'm going to end up contrasted with the unsettling feeling when evening approaches. I'm not entirely sure why this is. Even though I have everything I need to camp, there's something about being alone and in the dark that unnerves me. For many other travelers, this isn't the case. They're comfortable laying down anywhere at night. Even in my hitchhiking, backpacking, and car camping days, I prefer to be settled when darkness falls.

I cycle in and out of Lima having no reason to stay. In the town of Elida, I buy food for dinner, breakfast, some lunches, and snacks. As I get back on the bike, I'm starting to feel the long day. I've been riding since early morning, in the heat, with a lot of additional energy expended navigating. Once again, I decide to push it, Sirens be damned. Apparently, this is one lesson I will not learn. There's one campground within striking distance, 16 miles west in Middle Point. I should be fine.

I spend the next several miles riding past strip malls and car dealerships in what could be Anyplace, America. With a good shoulder, new pavement, and not too much traffic, my first afternoon and evening on the Lincoln Highway is smooth sailing. But it's growing late, and the darkness is due more to threatening clouds than the setting sun. Cycling on a flat, wind-free road, I'm flying across the plains. Nothing like a potential thunderstorm to get the adrenaline and legs cranking. After 8 miles, I reach Delphos, buy a drink and ponder the situation. I'm closing in on 100 miles today, and the campground is another 8 miles west. It's only 7 p.m., but the sky ahead looks ominous. So far, I've done well going for it, increasing my daily miles and putting me further west. What the hey, of course I cycle on.

It's growing even darker, cars have their headlights on, and I pedal faster. I see a drive-in movie theater ahead. That would be cool, to see a movie on my bike at a drive-in, but not with this weather. There it is, "Huggy Bear Campground Next Left." Oh my, this is no ordinary campground. First, I pass the RV sales with rows of new recreational vehicles, and then I make the left into Huggy Bear "City."

Paradise by the RV Lights

There are more people and far more action than most towns I've been through. I come to a lake with boats, rafts, and floats on my right, a pool straight ahead, a splash pad, kids on bikes, folks of all ages driving golf carts, and people walking within this RV wonderland. After riding miles through rural country, I feel like I'm on another planet. It's a cross between an amusement park and... I don't know what, but something I've never seen. I do know that these are not my peeps. They tour America in motorhomes with all the amenities known to modern humans. I'm the polar opposite; I'm tired, and I want to set up camp before the rain. I don't think I have to worry about the dark with the lights from their toys and rigs.

I check in at the office/store/restaurant and pay my fee for the right to stake my tent and use the bathroom; I don't need any electric or plumbing hookups. The guy at the counter gives me a map with an "X" on my site. As I pedal that way, a golf cart with two women pulls alongside. They introduce themselves as the resort manager and "permanent resident." They want to escort me to my site. Very sweet; you don't get this at a Motel 6. I'm never too tired to accept kindness and follow them along the road. At my site, I scope out the best spot for my tent and the pair of women return with a gift of banana and bottles of water. "Let us know if you need anything," they offer and let me know where they live.

I'm unloading gear from my bike when a guy comes over to the pick-up truck parked in my area. "Sorry for parking in your space," he says. "I can move it." I laugh, and pointing to my bike tell him, "Don't worry. I won't need the space."

He adds, "Come on over next door when you're done setting up. We're having a party."

Minutes later, my tent is up with the sleeping bag inside and pad inflated, I walk around the rigs and am warmly welcomed to a high school graduation party. I'm handed a Keystone Light, excellent after a long day cycling, and am introduced to 20 people from Ohio and

BIKING, LESSONS, BLESSINGS AND BEER

Michigan. "Eat," the ladies implore, "We have tons of food." They lead me to the shed where there's a smorgasbord of food: green bean casserole, macaroni salad, chips, potato salad, chicken, burgers. They apologize for having finished the corn on the cob. I fill my plate and join the others.

What is going on? I pedaled my brains out, beat the storm, camped in an RV wonderland, and am now being warmly welcomed by a group of people I just met. My oh my. Some of the family are regulars at this campground with their own pad—a storage shed atop concrete slab in addition to the RVs. They are quite the kind and incredibly generous group.

I spend most of the evening asking questions and listening to Herm's answers. Herm is the family patriarch and has been a farmer his whole life, like his father before him. He tells me he'd help his dad plow fields with horses before there were tractors.

As a University of Michigan alum, I gain some cred with the Michigan side of the family. Herm's son is an engineer for General Motors, and I pepper him with questions about his work and the future of new car technology. I drink, eat, and listen until I'm too tired to stay awake; it's been a long day. Even though I can't keep my eyes open and my body's exhausted, I don't sleep well. Kids are riding their bikes, golf carts are making loops, and vehicles come and go with lights shining on my tent late into the night, the price I pay for wanting to be around people. Yet I learn another lesson. *Be wary of stereotypes, like the ones I have held toward RVers.*

Indiana & Illinois

June 18, 2017

Middle Point, Ohio to Royal Center, Indiana – 114 miles

Today's Father's Day and I plan to treat myself to a yummy breakfast as soon as I come across a restaurant. As I pack my tent and gear, my next-door neighbor to the left emerges from his RV. I'm wearing my University of Michigan bike jersey for the first time in Ohio. I didn't dare until now but figure I'll be out of Buckeye country soon. I just hope I don't instigate road rage in my final 20 Ohio miles. As my neighbor and I talk, I find out that he's an Ohio State alumnus and he still brings me a cup of coffee. RVers!

After the coffee, I head out and aim for Indiana, my fifth state.

But even in the midst of all this flat farmland it's not that easy, get turned around and confused near the Ohio-Indiana border. In my defense, there's no river to cross, no "Welcome to Indiana" signs, just fields. I ask for directions at a stop sign and find out that I just need to make a right turn. Minutes later I pull into Monroeville, Indiana and there it is, the Blueberry Pancake House. The waitress takes me to my booth, and I pass a man wearing a red Indiana Hoosier sweatshirt.

"Hi," I greet him. "Do you think I can wear my Michigan bike jersey in Indiana? I just biked through Ohio and I didn't dare."

He chuckles. "Sure, we don't like anyone." I laugh with him. Soon I'm eating pancakes with bananas, chocolate sauce and whipped cream. It is delicious, although it's a bit odd with so many families around and me, alone, on Father's Day. A man comes over and sits across from me in my booth.

"I just want to say hi and see how's everything going," he says.

Huh? Oh, I remember I'm now back on an established Adventure Cycling route and Monroeville likely gets its share of long-distance bikers. From my appearance he must know I'm biking.

"I'm great," I tell him. "Thank you." What a kind gesture.

I finish the scrumptious pancakes, head outside, and am sitting on a bench outside to call my family when a woman approaches me. She's a reporter for the Monroeville weekly paper and she'd like to take my picture. Would I mind? Why not?

Father's Day breakfast in Monroeville

Thus far, Indiana is making for interesting riding. I cross a large dam providing expansive views, meander along winding roads, and through tiny villages. When I stop at a small convenience store in Denver to get something to eat and drink, there's a loaded bike with slick new panniers parked out front. It's the first self-supported biker I've seen in some time. It belongs to Jerry, who appears to be in his sixties and is from Rochester, New Hampshire. Jerry started his ride in Oregon, but the mountains kicked his butt, so he took a train further east and resumed his ride.

A lot of people ask me about my direction of travel, east to west. They wonder why I'm going west and hint that I'd be better off doing the opposite although none of them have done it. As a matter of fact, not one current or former cross-country bicyclist ever suggested either direction. I did my homework on this subject. While it seems most folks bike west to east, there aren't compelling reasons to do so. The main reason people give for this direction is the wind. Yes, the wind is more likely to come from the west, and this happens more often in the afternoon, but it also blows from the north, south, east, and it even changes during the same day. If you've flown from the west to the east, you know that it's much faster flying this direction due to strong westerly winds, but those are at 30,000 feet, and I'm not biking 6 miles above the ground. From what I know, there are more reasons to go east to west than vice versa:

1. Early in the summer, one may encounter snow or bitter cold in the taller western mountains, but this is very unlikely later in the summer, when I plan to be there.

2. A rider starting in the East will be in better physical shape by the time he or she has to ride up the long, high-elevation western passes.

3. Riding west means not biking into the morning sun and glare. Most of the time the sun is to your left, south. By the time the sun is in the west, it's evening and time to stop riding.

4. The number one reason I'm going east to west is that I need to go to California. That means, "Go west," not so-young-man.

* * *

Jerry asks if I've been using Warm Showers. Not yet, I tell him. I first heard of Warm Showers from my son. One of his college friends biked to California from Michigan the summer before and used Warm Showers, a combination of couchsurfing and Airbnb. It's an "organization" in which bicyclists and hosts create profiles and potential hosts can accept or reject a request to stay with them. After the stay, hosts and guests are reviewed. My profile has my plans for my trip and reads:

"I am a 54-year-old lifelong biker who started riding a tricycle, graduating to a Raleigh Chopper three speed, then a Schwinn Varsity ten speed, and am riding cross country on a Specialized Diverge. This summer I plan to pedal out my door in Vermont to see my daughter in California. I hope to make it at least to Montana where my son is living. I am married and have an incredible wife who supports this journey. I have been a teacher and principal for over 30 years and am currently head of school that educates students who have experienced complex trauma. We blend academics, experiential learning, and social/emotional well-being. I had dreamed of doing a cross-country bike ride since hearing about it in the 1970s from a neighbor."

Jerry from New Hampshire tells me how much he enjoys staying at Warm Showers' hosts. It's been the highlight of his trip. I tell him there haven't many hosts on my route up to now and how much difficulty I have using the website on my phone. Jerry, a decade older than me, shows me the app to download on my phone. I do and wow, a game changer.

I use the app to arrange my first Warm Showers for tonight with Frances in Royal Center, Indiana. For the first time in several days, I have a concrete destination. Fighting an intense headwind all afternoon, I roll west, often at the measly pace of 8 miles per hour. I'm back in farm country, immense fields in every direction. I pass some houses when I hear someone holler.

I head over to where a hulk of a man is standing in the yard in front of a house. He tells me he just hosted group of cyclists and offers me a place to stay for the night as well as "the best pizza I'll ever eat" from a nearby town. If you're thinking, "Man, this sounds creepy. Amos is biking by himself in the middle of Indiana. This could end up like a scene out of Deliverance." Let me assure you, it doesn't feel sketchy in the least. The guy is friendly, genuinely welcoming, and I have yet to experience a moment where I feel threatened by a person. As a matter of fact, the only negative interaction I've had was when that woman in Vermont flipped me the bird on day one. If I hadn't arranged a Warm Showers, I would have taken him up on his offer. Instead I thank him and tell him that I have a place to stay not far away.

Typical of how things have been going, the wind continues to be a force in the late afternoon. It's hard not to keep looking at the odometer with its depressing output. I still have 15 miles to go, I'm traveling 6, 7, 8 miles per hour when the wind is gusting and up to 10 when it lets up a bit. To add insult to injury, I can't blame the hills for my measly speed; the terrain is flat.

What truly astounds me is how I've taken to marking my "progress." When I ride I always measure my distance in miles. "Ten miles to the next town." "I've ridden 16 miles so far today." "I'm making good time averaging 15 miles per hour." Riding into this fierce headwind, I resort to measuring tenths of a mile. Tenths! Under ordinary circumstances this would be depressing, but these aren't normal times. The tenths of miles at least signify that I am making progress, however slowly.

I take a break for a snack and from the wind in Fletcher, an unincorporated town. I sit on the steps of a town building, the only structure here that's not a house, and hope that the trail mix provides a much-needed energy boost. I eat often to try to fend off the tiredness. A Clif bar, Poptart, bagel and peanut butter, trail mix, whatever I have left in my panniers. The afternoon is becoming evening, and I don't want to arrive at my host's too late. After my short break, I round a sharp corner and am up against the wind. I'm moving quite slowly when I see and hear two dogs barking like sons of bitches on my right. They're good size and look mean. Tired or not, my adrenaline kicks in. It's time for fight or flight; freezing is not an option. Up to now I've been lucky; this is my first canine confrontation. Man's best friend, yes. Biker's best friend? Not so much.

Riding into the stiff headwind, there's no way I'm gonna outrace them. There's also no way I'm going backwards. Fight it has to be. I yell at them, "Go home!" Nope, they keep coming. "Go home!" They don't listen worth a damn and no one comes out to rein them in. Fine, bring it on!

I dismount, grab my pump to use as a club, and roll the bike between me and the barking, snarling canines. "No!" I yell. "Go home!" Shielding myself with my bike, I stay on the left side of the road, they stay to my right, menacing, growling, and barking. I walk, wielding the pump, hoping a car might run interference. No luck. They continue baring their teeth, and I keep give them stern commands, which they ignore. They have yet to breach my defenses and I wonder how long this will go on. Then, without so much as a goodbye, they stop, turn, and retreat. Whew. I get back on my bike and start pedaling, drained even more.

A mile here, a right turn there, I know I have to be getting close. I spot something in the road ahead. As I near I see that it's faded white paint on the pavement spelling "Water ahead." A half mile later I make out more words on the pavement, "Bikers welcome." Then

BIKING, LESSONS, BLESSINGS AND BEER

I'm outside a farmhouse surrounded by Indiana cornfields. The numbers on the mailbox tell me I've reached the address of my Warm Showers host.

I ride up the short driveway, dismount, and prop my bike against the back deck. I have no idea what to expect. "Helloooo…" I call out.

A spry, 80-year-old woman emerges the house. I figure she's one of my hosts here in Royal Center, Indiana, population 661. Turns out she's Frances, my only host. There's no one else, just Frances. Who does this, takes a stranger into her house in 2017? We introduce ourselves, chat a bit, and she directs me to my room and the shower. My first warm shower, phenomenal.

Hoosier hospitality at Frances's home

After I'm clean and changed, I head downstairs and hang with Frances, an Indiana Hoosier through and through. Widowed, she and her husband once farmed corn and soy, and she tells me they had a small hog operation, 1,800 piggies. Now she lives alone, but most of her eight kids and 35 grandkids aren't far away. Frances leads me to a gigantic barn where they once stored farm machinery; tonight, it will house my bike. I lean my bike against a freezer, and we head back to the house just before it starts pouring, perfect timing.

Fifteen minutes later Frances and I head back outside to view a rainbow arcing over the fields in front of her house. As she prepares dinner, I ask if there's anything I can do to help. A light bulb's out at the top of the stairs so I get a step ladder and change it. There's a certain warmth and formality about Frances and she loves talking about her kids and grandkids. Some are university scholarship athletes at Purdue and Indiana; I listen and keep asking questions. We have an easy rapport and I feel comfortable in my new friend's home.

Frances is great company and I enjoy a delicious home cooked dinner, dessert, and a jar of M&M's to snack on as I help with dishes. I ask Frances how she became a host. She tells me she's not a biker, but her son did a bike trip a few years back, she was intrigued by his stories and she signed up. He's the one whom I communicated with by text although he doesn't live here. Frances doesn't text. She tells me she enjoys hosting cyclists, and while her friends think she is crazy to do this, she laughs, "I'm not worried about bikers stealing my television and riding away with it."

June 19, 2017

BIKING, LESSONS, BLESSINGS AND BEER

Royal Center to Rensselaer, Indiana – 72 miles

Although not one to usually eat breakfast, I try to be a gracious guest, so this morning I dine on eggs and fruit with Frances before saying goodbye. I've just slept in the home of a complete stranger where I enjoyed a shower, dinner, breakfast, and excellent company. If this is what Warm Showers is like, I'm hooked. I also realize that if an 80-year-old widow in the middle of nowhere can open her home to others, I surely can do this too.

My first stop of the day is a gas station and store in Brook, Indiana where I buy snacks. I plan to hang in the town library for a work phone call at 10 a.m. Libraries are heavenly with their internet, bathrooms, cold water, and air conditioning. I sit at a computer and at 10 Central Time, call work. The touch screen on my phone isn't responding. I shut down the phone, restart it, and wait. The screen stays dark. Using the computer, I find troubleshooting pages for the Samsung Galaxy. I have to reinstall the system, likely losing all apps and data on the phone. I don't see many other options, so I do it. I anxiously wait for the phone to install the new system, start up, and work. Meanwhile I email my boss and tell her about my phone mishap. Eventually the phone restarts and the screen still doesn't work.

In everyday life I don't think I'm overly reliant or connected to a cell phone, but this trip is anything but typical. The cell phone's a vital tool. It helps me make arrangements for getting my tent, meeting Annie and Lori, and locating motels and campgrounds. It's my connection to my wife and kids, my map when I'm not on Adventure Cycling routes, my source for weather forecasts, and now it's how I connect with Warm Showers hosts. After all, I haven't seen a pay phone on a street corner in years.

Since libraries are few and far between, open limited hours, and the only places I know where I can access computers, having a phone is a big deal. The cell phone is the Swiss army knife for a transcontinental biker.

I ask the librarian if she knows where I can deal with my phone. She tells me of a place 25 miles north and off route, or there's a store in Rensselaer, 20 miles east from where I just came. Both are awful options, the idea of backtracking especially. Ride east when I'm headed west? That's hard to swallow, but I know the route from where I came, the road's good, and the wind will be at my back in the afternoon. Backtracking east it will be.

I email Jeannie, Hannah, and Jake to tell them I'll be without a cell phone indefinitely in case they try to reach me. If and when I get the phone fixed today, it'll be mid-afternoon, hot, and with strong headwinds so staying the night in Rensselaer makes sense. I send an

BIKING, LESSONS, BLESSINGS AND BEER

email to Rensselaer's one Warm Showers host to ask if he can host me. I let him know that my phone's on the fritz so email's the only way to reach me.

I eat an especially leisurely lunch in Brook's town park near the library as I'm in absolutely no hurry. Then I bike, fly really, back to Rensselaer. Flat terrain and a tailwind mean that without working too hard I ride at a pace of 18 miles per hour and love it.

The phone store's located on the main drag and easy to find. I lock my bike and head in. As my sweaty, scrufty self enters the store, a young, bearded, phone salesman greets me.

"Amos?" he asks.

Huh? How's he know my name? Weird and also intriguing. I only told my family that I lost my phone.

"How do you know my name?" I ask, somewhat accusingly.

"Chris called."

"Huh?" I wondered aloud.

"The guy you are staying with..."

"Ohhh." Now I get it. Chris is the Warm Showers host whom I emailed, have not met, and don't even know if he would host me. He called the store and told Steffen, the salesman, that I may show up. How did Chris even know I'd be at this store? Sure, Rensselaer, Indiana is not Chicago, but with 6,000 people and the only sizable city around, it could have multiple places that sold phones. Very odd.

Steffen takes a look at my phone and does the same things I tried with the same futile results. I'll be buying another phone today. As I'm looking over phones, guess who come into the store? Chris, my host for the night. He's checking to see if I'm okay, asks if I need anything, and if I want him to give me a ride to his house. Wow. More Hoosier hospitality. Since it's mid-afternoon, I thank Chris for his kind offer, and tell him that I'll be over later that afternoon as I have some errands to run.

Steffen, the phone rep, shows me options for phones, and I buy the cheapest I can find, a newer version of my Galaxy. Steffen sets up the new phone and tells me about himself. He dreams of a career in music and has a goal to learn two instruments a year.

"Can I have your business card?" I ask Steffen. "I want to write your superiors to commend your work."

"Thanks," he replies, "but there's no need. I'm moving to St. Louis next week for a job with a recording studio." Good for him.

The phone store doesn't have a case to fit my phone, so I head to my second Walmart of the trip. I have no idea what I need and ask a young employee for help. I tell him what I'm doing, and I learn about him and his young family. Another employee joins in and the two of them are cracking jokes. Never had so much fun in a Walmart. Not long ago I had a broken phone, was riding east instead of west, had no idea where I would be staying, and now I'm all set; better,

BIKING, LESSONS, BLESSINGS AND BEER

really.

Since I told Chris that I'll be at his house around 6, I have time to kill. I hang out on the shady lawn in front of the courthouse for a bit and then decide to check out a bike shop, that according to the Adventure Cycling notes, is on route. I can't find it. My directions take me to the address but there's no shop. I call their number and they tell me that the store's moved and give me directions to a tractor shop up the road. After 25 years, the bike shop is no more. What remains are bike tools within a small room in the tractor store. I've heard that fewer kids are riding bikes, primarily due to parents' fears. That's a shame; biking meant freedom and exploring for both me and my kids. Another example of the growth of the nanny state and wimpification of our country.

I try to find Chris's house hiding in plain sight in a new, cookie-cutter subdivision, but pass his road several times. The third time's the charm and it doesn't matter that I added extra miles in the heat. I have a place to sleep and all the time in the world.

Chris and his wife, Jodi, are sweet, giving people, and certainly not long-distance bikers; they don't own bikes. They're Warm Showers hosts because they enjoy hearing the stories of bicyclists, and I get the sense they just enjoy giving. Close to me in age, Chris was laid off from the recently closed local college. Still, he's hosting me. He now drives a school bus. Jodi works at a grocery store and they both are part-time Methodist ministers. They have a friendly rescue dog who they tell me is normally anxious and takes prozac. Antidepressants for dogs. I'm again given a room and a bathroom of my own. I take a shower and the three of us drive down the road to a local pizza joint whose decor reminds me of Pizza Hut. I'd like a beer, but since they're drinking pop and treating, I too opt for soda from the fountain. While they're not the preaching type, I'm usually of the "When in Rome do as the Romans do" mindset. So, pop it is and again, I'm grateful for such hospitality.

From the home of a retired and widowed grandma farmer in an iconic Indiana farmhouse to a childless couple in a cookie-cutter subdivision on the same day. I've been welcomed with open arms into homes of people I would never have met, much less slept and dined under their roofs had I not been on the voyage. This is amazing! After dinner, Chris and Jodi settle down to watch CSI on their giant television. I watch for a bit and then bid them goodnight.

As native Hoosier son John Mellencamp sang in Pink Houses:
"Oh, but ain't that America for you and me,
Ain't that America somethin' to see baby,
Ain't that America home of the free,
Little pink houses for you and me."

BIKING, LESSONS, BLESSINGS AND BEER

June 21, 2017

Rennselaer, Indiana to Wenona, Illinois – 115 miles

Chris gets up early with me the next morning and kindly brews me coffee. I enjoy a cup with him and it's back to Brook.

I make the trip without a map; it's my third time biking this section. I stop at the same convenience store as yesterday, but because it's earlier in the morning, there's a group of guys sitting at tables in the adjoining room. I ask if I could join them and they make room for me.

I wouldn't consider doing this back home, but on the road, it's becoming a morning ritual. The conversations connect me to where I am and are usually good for some laughs. The guys, always guys, almost all older than me, are typically less curious about me than I am about them. These gents tell me about their community, the exodus of young folks, and the amazing changes in agricultural technology, like how kids in high school are using drones to monitor crops. I tell them about my phone and how this is my second visit to Brook in 2 days. When they hear that I'm going west, everyone chimes in, prompting a 15-minute explanation of how to best get out of Brook. The road crew's working up ahead, so the road is torn up. They discuss my options and which detour to take in elaborate and complicated detail. Even though I'm only 10 or so miles from the Illinois border, getting out of Indiana is proving to be a challenge. I try to write down their directions on my phone, but I can't keep up. They can't provide many landmarks in corn country. With road names like S 275 W, W 700 S, County Rd 825 S and 300 W, I'm lost before I start.

"You'll find it," they assure me. I thank them, ride the car-free rural roads named with letters and numbers and when I see the fairgrounds, I know I've gotten there. I made an enormous horseshoe. In Iroquois, I stop in the grocery store whose shelves are mostly bare and devoid of anything fresh, call the convenience store in Brook and ask the store clerk to let the farmers know I made it. Then I enter the only place open to eat, a bar. I have breakfast next to old timers, but there's not much chatter while they watch tv. A guy sitting next to me is wearing a Bud Light cap and has two empty cans of Busch Light in front of him. Maybe I should offer to treat. I look at my watch. It's 9 a.m.

With eggs, coffee, and water in me, but no beer, I hit the road. I ride through an Illinois countryside that looks a lot like Indiana. My next stop is for a bite to eat and liquid refreshment at the highway intersection in Ashkum. I'm unlocking my bike when a man walks over and asks, "Do you need a place to stay?" He tells me about camping in the town park. His name is Paul, he's the mayor, and the keeper of the restroom key for camping at Ashkum Village Park. I

BIKING, LESSONS, BLESSINGS AND BEER

remember that the Adventure Cycling maps mentioned both the park and him. Quite the coincidence. It's early in the day so I thank him for the offer and pedal on and on and on through the Illinois countryside.

* * *

Later that morning I meet Al, or I should say, he meets me. He's riding his bike the other way, does a U-turn when he sees me, and rides alongside. There are few cars on this road so we bike side by side. Somewhere on my trip I heard the following: Riding solo people find you approachable and less threatening. Riding as a pair, you're still not very threatening, but less approachable. In a group of three or more it's unlikely that strangers choose to interact with you.

Illinois Al's out for a pleasure ride. He rode cross-country with a friend several years back, also east to west. He tells me of another advantage—not worrying about cars getting blinded by the morning sun by going west. He also says that he wanted to go west as that was the way the country was settled. I never thought of that. Al rides with me for a half hour until we reach a store and his cut-off. He treats me to coffee and is off. What a pleasant diversion.

Illinois Al

Around here they're farming corn and soy for animal feed, corn for ethanol, and wind for electricity. In spite of the omnipresent sun, I don't see a single solar panel. During one of my breakfasts with farmers, I ask what they do after planting and before harvesting. "Nowadays, equipment's too complicated to work on. With all the modified crops and pesticides, there's not much to do." That's why, they tell me, I see guys mowing strips of grass along the road: something to do. "Corn, soy, then 2 months in Miami," was their motto once upon a time.

I keep on going, stopping for a break at the library in Streator, and in the evening decide to splurge on a room at America's Best Value Inn off Interstate 39. It's been a long day. I cook dinner on my stove outside the motel using the wall as a windbreak.

BIKING, LESSONS, BLESSINGS AND BEER

June 22, 2017

Wenona to Cambridge, Illinois – 75 miles

I wake to a gorgeous Illinois morning, perfect for cycling. The sun is glorious, not yet hot, and there's only a slight breeze. I cycle through corn and soy fields and usually have the road to myself for long stretches. Sometimes I ride on the left just because I can. Occasionally I stop to check road signs, at times venture off route, but not too far, never too lost. I've found my rhythm and I'm in the zone. All's well in the world. Then I feel a snap when I shift. Uh oh, this isn't good. I click on the shifter, no tension, no shifting. Before looking, I'm sure what it is, a broken derailleur cable. I pull behind a shed out of the sun to take a look. Yep, the cable's broken inside the shifter. I'm about 4 miles from Kewanee. I'll bike there and then see what I can do.

I ride there in the hardest gear and stop at one of the omnipresent gas station-convenience stores, fill my water bottles with ice from the soda machine, and eat a few chocolate pop tarts. Then I take a look at the derailleur and cable. Not good. It snapped underneath the brake in the handlebar. I know from experience that this is not a simple fix, even if I were carrying an extra cable, which I'm not. My first real issue and I haven't even had a flat yet. I use my phone and Google bike shops in the area. The nearest one is in Peoria, 50 miles north and a long way off route. I wonder about hitching a ride. It won't be easy with all my stuff, but maybe if I ask someone at the gas station with a pick-up. Would anyone be going to Peoria, and what if they are only going part way? Then I'd be stranded, and it could be a long time hitching. At least Kewanee is a small city. Better to figure out things here.

I consider other options. What about a taxi? Can a taxi take my bike? Plus, I'm cheap and that would be one expensive taxi ride. Riding 50 miles with my gears the way they are seems impossible. The derailleur defaulted to the hardest gear in both the front and rear chainring, I'm not sure what my best option is, yet I stay calm. This is a good sign. No need to panic. What would that do? And there's no one here to bail me out.

I've been intentionally aiming for around 100 miles a day when all is favorable for just this reason, so I can take time off when I want or when the weather's bad. Or when a cable breaks. I call Omer and Bob's, my bike shop back home. Sam, one of the mechanics who coincidentally enjoys touring, answers, and I explain the situation.

"You've got to take it to a shop," he commands. "You won't be able to fix that on the road." "The nearest bike shop is over 50 miles away. What can I do to make it rideable?" I ask. Sam suggests that I set the adjuster screws to lock the chain into mid-range gears, and that's what I do. I have fourth and 11th gears to pedal me to Muscatine, about 80 miles away but on route. I figure I'll do some today and the rest tomorrow. Thank goodness I'm in mostly flat Illinois, just rolling hills with nothing remotely resembling a mountain.

West towards Muscatine it is. The pedaling is slower and harder, but the wind isn't bad and I'm doing okay coasting when I can and standing when I need to. It's late in the hot afternoon when I bike 2 miles off route to the Old Timber Campgrounds. I especially don't want to add miles now, so I called ahead to make sure they are open and have space. They are and do; I have yet to come to an RV campground that can't or won't squeeze in a tent and bike, but I never want the extra miles to go for naught. For all I know, they could be closed.

Since I've had good experiences in private campgrounds thus far, I roll up in good spirits, 20 miles closer to Muscatine and a bike shop. A group of folks is sitting in chairs, lounging in the shade in front of the office. All is mellow so I sit down and ask, "What do you guys do for fun?"

"There's a cribbage tournament tonight," someone says, in all seriousness. I gotta learn cribbage. Betty, the owner takes me inside the store/office, I pay the $10 to camp and join the group on the porch.

"Is there any cold beer around?" I ask no one in particular. As a guy pulls away in his pick-up, Betty yells, "Earl!"

Earl slams on the brakes and Betty grabs a Coors Light from a cooler in the bed of the truck and hands it to me. I crack it open—cold and delicious.

When I finish my beer, I follow Betty in her golf cart, me on my bike, to my campsite. First, she stops at the bathroom to tells me that this area is prone to tornadoes and the restroom is the emergency shelter. The sign on the wall says the same thing. I don't bother to tell her that I have experience sleeping in park bathrooms.

I set up my tent in the middle of the central lawn, not directly under any trees and walk to the pond. It's about 5 p.m., 80 degrees, sunny, an absolutely spectacular day, and there's no one around. Eventually Collette and her son, whom I met on the porch, also enjoy the pond. I swim, lounge in the sun, and make calls to two teachers who are considering not returning to school that fall. This is the life.

* * *

As I cook dinner that evening, I'm in good spirits. I handled the setback of a broken cable just fine, rode well, and had time to enjoy a beautiful setting. Just as I'm thinking it can't get any better, Collette and her son show up in their golf cart with a delivery—a 12-pack of Bud Lights in a cooler. Twelve? I'm blown away by this gesture. I thank her profusely. But 12? Not knowing how many to take, but knowing a dozen is way too many, I snag four and leave her the rest.

Tastes great. Less filling.

Later a man stops by, points to his RV, and tells me that if a storm rolls in, I'm welcome to stay on his porch. Then I cook dinner in a fire ring, thoroughly enjoy two Bud Lights, appreciating that light beer can be much more refreshing than water. The next morning, I bring the cooler and two leftover beers to the deck outside Collette's camper.

This past winter, I planted the seed for this trip, and in the spring, I started to water it. I read several books about cross-country trips, looked at routes, and researched bikes. The bike I had, a Specialized Tarmac, is too light, not built to carry panniers, and the geometry is not suited for being in the saddle for 100 miles day after day. In April, after months of deliberating, I finally bought a bike that could carry me across country, a Specialized Diverge. With that purchase, I committed. I joined Adventure Cycling, read cyclists' posts, and considered routes. It was game on.

While many thought I was meshugana, the only ones who expressed worry were my 80-year-old parents. This trip seemed pretty tame compared to some of my past adventures. One night in late spring my mother left a message on my voicemail telling me she had an offer. She didn't say what it was. I was intrigued and called her back.

"We'd like to buy you a plane ticket," my mother said.

"Okay," I answered.

She continued, "What if we bought you a ticket to Denver and then you biked from there?" Huh?

"But then I wouldn't be biking across country," I responded. Obviously, I didn't accept their gift. Tonight, I'm camping in Illinois.

Iowa

June 23, 2017

Cambridge, Illinois to Iowa City, Iowa – 76 miles

I have 60 miles of quite a bit slower than normal, two-gear riding this morning to get to Muscatine and the bike shop. While waiting at the traffic light in Orion, I ask a cab driver where I can find good ice cream. He tells me there's a Dairy Queen down the road a ways. I ask if there's anything closer and he points to the McDonald's across the street. Riding with only two gears and now even hotter in town, I ignore previous lessons and go to McD's where I order a vanilla ice cream cone, the only choice.

I relax in a booth and enjoy the cold water and bland, albeit chilly ice cream. It's quiet, a couple of middle-aged employees sit in the adjacent booth, and we talk. They seem to have some different abilities and are quite content working here. While we talk, the manager comes over and hands me a mango smoothie. It is scrumptious. There must be a lesson here.

Temporarily rejuvenated from the treats and cool air of Mickey D's, I resume pedaling west. Forty more miles to go before I reach Harpers Cycling and Fitness in Muscatine, Iowa. First, I cross the gateway to the West, the mighty Mississippi River. I'm underwhelmed by its tameness. What did we do to this once wild and magnificent waterway? Tom and Huck would be cussing.

After I cross the famed waterway, a sign lets me know that the people of Iowa welcome me. Not the governor or just an impersonal "Welcome to Iowa," but the people themselves. Fantastic. I've reached my seventh state and more importantly, a city with a bike shop. Since all I have for directions is a state highway map of Iowa, it's up to Google Maps to lead me. It directs me along the Mississippi River on a road that's closed for construction. Zigzagging through Muscatine, my two gears and I eventually make it to Harpers Cycling and Fitness where I hope they can fix my derailleur now. Worse case scenario, I'll spend the night in Muscatine.

The young buck mechanic is super helpful and is able to get the cable out, not an easy task even for him as it's broken and frayed. He

BIKING, LESSONS, BLESSINGS AND BEER

notices the play in my chain and using the guide tool, convinces me that the chain needs replacing. It's likely due to my standing and putting extra stress on it and, with over 3,000 miles left on my tour, I think it's worth it. With extreme appreciation towards my new friends at Harpers, an hour and a half later I'm on my way out of Muscatine and on to Iowa City where I have a Warm Showers awaiting.

There are lots of hosts in Iowa City, and I'm learning to read profiles and look for those who seem most interesting. Typically hosts are older, most are bicyclists, and many have toured. Because I don't usually plan far in advance and I'm not guaranteed an immediate response, often I text a few folks to see who might be able to host me. I choose Jim in Iowa City whose blurb reads,

"If you are on a long distance tour and would like a nice bed to sleep in, shower, and laundry, give us a shout. We are avid bikers, and have done some long tours across country and through New Zealand, and enjoy racing too. We can offer a quiet place for you to rest or take you bicycling around Iowa City to show you local attractions. We are friends with the owners/managers of all the local shops in town, and can help you with bike repairs too. We don't have pets, the house is no smoking, and our max group size would be 4, but prefer 1 or 2. You can use the kitchen, we could go out to eat, grill, or cook whatever your craving. We would

prefer 1 or 2 night stays not longer unless an agreement is worked out. You may also enjoy sharing your story with our teenage boy Sebastian!"

The guys at Harpers bike shop give me directions out of Muscatine. I think I understand, kinda, but apparently do not because as soon as I ride away from the shop I'm confused. I default to Google Maps which puts me on a bike path. Excellent, I think. Bike paths avoid automobiles and trucks, especially welcome in a city, but they're often less direct, have worse pavement, frequent stops and thus I don't go as fast as I do on the road. I'm eager to get moving as the day's growing late.

I follow the bike path leading me into a tremendous park-school complex. I continue following the Google voice telling me where to turn until I reach an enormous fence blocking my way. There's no exit. I'm trapped. The spiked fence is way too tall to hoist over my 55-pound, loaded bike. I have to backtrack, and I am not happy. Finally, I find a way out and onto a busy road, a long uphill, into the wind, three of the six deadly sins. A tough day is getting tougher.

I head west and north using the state map and Google Maps, which are nowhere near as detailed or helpful as the Adventure Cycling maps. It's impossible to get a sense of scale on the state map, road names don't match what Google Maps show on my phone, there are no stores, and few people outside the scattered houses. I figure as long as I head north and west, I'm going the right way. The wind blows stronger, I'm more tired and I still have 40 miles until Iowa City. I ought to have stayed in Muscatine. Too late for that.

I don't think I'm lost, but I definitely don't know where I am. I have no landmarks for references. I pass a few state fishing access areas, but they aren't on my map and I keep pedaling. Construction signs intermittently line the road. They're in the process of repairing the road so the pavement's a mess, the workers are gone for the day.

Tired? Check. Strong headwinds? Double check. Poor road? Check. When I come to an intersection with a stop sign, I pull over. I'm losing energy fast. Cars stop at the intersection, but no one asks me if I'm okay or need anything. Yeah, I need a lift, thanks for asking.

I've been moving at about 8 miles per hour, slower when the wind gusts. I still have 20 miles to go and should make it to Iowa City by dark. I call Jim to tell him I'll be there, but late. When he asks where I am, I tell him I'm approaching Lone Tree, Jim says it's only a 15-minute ride by car from his house; he'll come to get me when his partner gets home. Woo hoo!

Then Jim says to me, "Ride into Lone Tree, and when you get into town and start heading downhill, there's a bar on the left. I'll meet you there."

I would have been happy stopping and waiting for him at that intersection; instead, I slog on and then I see it: the water tower in the distance. "Beware the Lone Tree water tower," Jim had warned. "No matter how long you ride, the water towers in the midwest never seem to get closer." They're like desert mirages.

Jim's right. Moving as slowly as I am, the 5 miles from when I spot the water tower until I reach the Lone Tree city limit sign takes forever. Eventually the speed limit drops from 55 miles per hour to 40 and down to 30 mph, and I know I made it. My energy surges. Beer! I pump hard up the hill knowing the bar is on the other side. I crest the hill, eyes peeled for the upcoming bar when I hear, "Amos!" I look to my right and see a guy beckoning to me from the BP gas pumps. I head over. It's Jim and he's holding a plastic bag. Inside are a bottle of water, Gatorade, and an All-Day IPA.

"I didn't know which you'd want, so I got all three," he tells me, passing me the bag. Who does this, for a stranger no less?

"Beer, please and thank you," I say smiling. This is going to be a good visit.

Courtesy counts. I was only calling Jim to let him know I'd be late, seemed like the right thing to do. In response, he saves my arse.

Jim's car assist is the first ride I've received that actually shortened my biking, by 15 miles, and I couldn't care less. I didn't dip my tire in the Atlantic Ocean either. I gave up being a purist decades ago.

Jim describes the environs as we drive to his house where I meet his partner, Lisa. I immediately feel at home among friends. They're

BIKING, LESSONS, BLESSINGS AND BEER

full of warmth, energy, and humor. This is my third homestay, and while the other two were hosted by generous and kind folks, we didn't have enough in common to become friends.

I shower, settle in, and soon a bunch of Jim and Lisa's friends join us for a cookout on the deck. I have a blast with these guys as they joke incessantly. I listen, observe, occasionally chime in, and enjoy. I go to bed around 11 while the party's still rocking. It's like my time with the youngsters at Blue Mountain Lake, except these folks are more like me, albeit still a bit younger.

It doesn't take long for me to be comfortable enough with Jim and Lisa that the next morning I ask if I could spend another night with them. An off-day in Iowa City seems like a good plan. Resting in Columbus re-energized me physically and emotionally, provided my body a chance to chill, not having to look for another place to stay, and not having to think about my stuff. Jim and Lisa are happy to oblige; they like having me here.

June 24, 2017

Iowa City, Iowa

Unlike the off day with my cousin in Columbus, this is no zero day. Jim and Lisa bike. We don't get in the car today, we don't walk, and we don't stay home. All day and night we zoom around Iowa City by bike. We ride on city bike paths and along neighborhood streets. I feel light and free on my first day riding without gear. Plus, I'm a bike tourist with the best local guides. First, Jim and I bike into town where I get groceries and mail more stuff back home. Later, we bike to the farmer's market and then to a neighborhood party for a Nigerian man who just became a U.S. citizen. Very cool, especially with the anti-immigrant rhetoric spouted by this president. In the evening, Lisa, Jim, and I bike into town again for an inaugural, city-wide street festival. At one point I cut away and am treated to a barbecue dinner with the parents of one of my daughter's good friends who live here in Iowa City. How great is this? On the way home that night we stop by a friend's for another beer. What a day. I'm a tourist who's beginning to feel like a local.

I'm having a super fun time with Jim and Lisa, making new friends, and recharging before continuing west. As I pack in the guest room to get ready for tomorrow morning's departure, Jim and Lisa ask if I want to join them tomorrow for a beer ride in Pella. I have no idea what a "beer ride" is but figure when in Iowa, do as the Iowans. Sure, I'd be glad to. We'll spend Sunday night with Jim's college roommate and then I'll go west on Monday.

June 25, 2017

Pella, Iowa – 70 miles

After coffee and breakfast, we load the bikes and drive to Pella, an hour and half away. At Pat's house Jim, Lisa, and Pat drink a "breakfast beer." I decline; I have to pace myself. I love biking and I love beer, but in the morning, before a bike ride, and with these guys? Jim competes in international cyclocross, and wins.

We're here to join a monthly pre-RAGBRAI (Register's Annual Great Bicycle Ride Across Iowa) ride. Today's event is the Peace Tree Brewing Company-Peanut Pub bike ride, whatever that means. I have no idea what to expect and am going with the flow. I do know that the RAGBRAI is an annual ride across Iowa that takes a different west to east route each year and is the world's largest bike-touring event. It's been happening for 45 years with between 10,000 and 20,000 riders annually, biking and drinking their way across the state. I plan to be well west of Iowa when this year's ride takes place. I suppose this is my small way of participating.

It's a gorgeous day to ride. We got a late start so after a hard warm-up, we catch the Peace Tree bus 10 miles from Kelly and Pat's house just as it's ready to roll out. It's the beer bus, and the folks working provide us with bottles of Peace Tree beers. Thirsty after pedaling hard, I enjoy my first beer of the morning, a Peace Tree "No Coast IPA" while Lisa, Jim, and Pat drink their second.

Next, it's onto Knoxville, home of Peace Tree Brewing Company and Tap Room for a break and my second beer, a Red Rambler. Peace Tree is sponsoring the ride and their beer mighty tasty and refreshing. Soon we're back in the saddle, waving at the passing beer bus as we bike back to Pella. We catch up to the bus where it's parked and have another beer. Instead of typical snack breaks, I'm stopping every so often for a beer. This is a ride unlike any other, cruising with good folks, drinking yummy beer, and I'm loving riding without carrying any weight. The terrain is rolling, the sun is shining and we're all having a good time.

BIKING, LESSONS, BLESSINGS AND BEER

At Peace Tree Brewing Company with Lisa, Jim, and Pat

We ride back to Pella, eat lunch, drink more beer, and play dice games with the bus driver, brewery employees, and other riders at the Peanut Pub. Then it's back to Knoxville, no rest for the thirsty. We catch the bus and make another beer stop. I chat with the beer crew and some of the riders, whom I'm getting to know better with each brew. Beer number four is delicious and hoppy and we continue back to Peace Tree Brewing for snacks and more beer, number five at the brewery. You get the idea. We all have good buzzes and I'm glad to not to have to worry about anything except pedaling. Since the bus is done for the day, I assume we're done drinking. Silly me. Jim and Pat head to a store as we prepare to depart. Half-way back to Pella we stop at a river park for a break and a drink. They bought more beer at the store.

We make our final approach to Pella as evening falls and stop for a Mexican dinner with the rest of Pat's family. Instead of beer, it's margaritas. After dinner I follow the others from the restaurant back to Pat and Kelly's, darkness falling as we reach the subdivision. Lisa passes me on my right, makes a left turn in front of me to the driveway and catches my front wheel. I skid to the pavement, skinning and bruising my leg. My first wipe out. A case of BUI (biking under the influence)? As I lay on the pavement recovering from the shock of the fall, no one checks to see how I am. I suppose that either means I am tough enough to hang with them, or they fall a lot and it's no big deal. Eventually I get up, bring my bike into the garage, and we settle in the living room to watch the Cardinals baseball game. Jim and Lisa have another beer and I bid them goodnight in order to strike out early and on my own the next morning.

June 26, 2017

Pella to Perry, Iowa – 101 miles

It's dark and raining hard as I pack my bike in Pat's garage. I'm going to wait at least for the rain to let up. Departing from a comfortable place on a beautiful day fills me with feelings of opportunity and optimism. Leaving new friends on a dark morning into the great unknown does not fill me with glee. And soon it will

BIKING, LESSONS, BLESSINGS AND BEER

get worse.

I'm up before the others and assume that they will rise late after yesterday's indulgences. Or not; their tolerance was impressive. I don my rain gear, turn on my headlight and taillight, and venture into town. I stop in a beautiful cafe with interior brick walls and photos of the way it was 70 years ago. I chat with the young barista as she prepares my coffee, look over the front page of the local newspaper on the counter, and proceed to make an insulting comment about Trump.

"I voted for Trump," she says curtly. Dang, I blew it. I'm not in Vermont. Young people working in upscale coffee shops (in Iowa at least) are not necessarily progressive. I apologize but the damage is done. Up until now, I've refrained from talking politics. Dummy! I pedal out of town in the drizzling dawn darkness, aware that I don't understand the directions my friends gave me last night. You know, me and directions. *When am I going to learn to write them down?* Google Maps, here we go.

Pissing off the barista creates bad karma

I'm taken to a highway on-ramp. Since this is a "recommended" bike route, I figure it's gonna lead to a chill state highway. I ride down the on-ramp and merge with a highway that's anything but calm. The road has two lanes in both directions with Monday morning rush hour traffic zipping by to boot. So much for a bike route; this feels downright dangerous. I consider turning around but going the opposite way up the on-ramp in the dark, rainy morning seems like an even worse idea. Better to ride to the first exit. The riding can't be that bad and it can't be too far.

It's worse. The shoulder is dirt. What am I going to do? I ride the dirt shoulder. What choice do I have? I cycle as fast and as far to the right as I dare and hope for the best. It's harrowing; cars zooming by in the light rain, their lights on, and me, riding on dirt with my thin tires. In 3 miles I come an exit. I reach the turn off but see that it's not an off-ramp but a church driveway. I don't give a damn; I'm getting off this road.

BIKING, LESSONS, BLESSINGS AND BEER

"It's a death trap, it's a suicide rap, we gotta get out while we're young..." I hear you, Mr. Springsteen, but I'm no longer young.

There's a road beyond the church which doesn't connect to the church. I'm not getting back on the highway, so I walk my bike hundreds of yards across a field to the road. It's one of Iowa's infamous gravel roads. Some people own gravel bikes especially for this terrain; I'm not one of those people. I figure it can't be too far until I hit pavement. After all, I just left the City of Pella.

Without the sun (or compass) to orient me west, I rely on Google Maps, but I'm disoriented. It all looks the same: the fields, the gravel roads, and although the gravel's much easier than sand, it's much harder to ride than pavement. When I come to another all-gravel intersection, I listen to Google and ride on. At the next intersection I notice the road name, look at Google Maps, and deduce that I made a big U. Karma. I'm certain it's payback for my interaction with the barista. After an hour of riding on this crap, I hit pavement, still not sure where to go.

I get to the town of Monroe, where at a convenience store, a few helpful folks set me in the right direction. Of course they do. Where am I going anyway? My next waypoint is Walden, Colorado where I'll pick up the TransAmerica Adventure Cycling Route and follow it to Missoula to see my sonny boy, Jake. Other than that, I intend to go as straight as I can across Iowa and Nebraska. Folks suggested I avoid riding through Des Moines so I will veer north.

Navigating on my own has its ups and downs. Sometimes I like making decisions, being spontaneous. But there's a downside—highways and gravel. The rest of the day, Google Maps put me on and off bike trails, and Iowa is full of them. Bike trails are a welcome respite from cars, even if they are slower going. The highlight of the trails today is the High Trestle Trail near Madrid (pronounced Mad Rid; we are in Iowa). The trail is busy with lots of folks walking, a cross country team running and folks out for an afternoon bike ride. The trestles themselves are an engineering feat.

I've ridden another 100-plus mile day as I approach Perry, a city with 7,000 people. Google Maps shows me the location of a motel and then, using their bike maps, I find myself back on dirt. Unbelievable. I switch to the car map which puts me on a busy highway, at dusk no less. No way I'm putting myself on that, so I switch back to the bike map and ride the roundabout dirt road. I find a motel in Perry as darkness sets in. With no restaurants within walking distance and not wanting to bike around at night, I cook dinner in my room, couscous and melted cheese. About as appetizing as it sounds, but quick and nutritious.

BIKING, LESSONS, BLESSINGS AND BEER

The Trestle Trail near Mad-rid

I head to the lobby the next morning where there's not even a real breakfast set-up. I snag some packaged danishes for snacks later and eat peanut butter and toast.

June 27, 2017
Perry to Onawa, Iowa – 120 miles

I'm deep into the Heartland. I ride through one small town after another, most not having much more than a post office, maybe a bank, garage, and a bar, or two. There are several ways of knowing when I'm approaching a town, because I usually don't realize it until I'm in it. The first is by noting how many miles it is on the map and gauging my odometer, but that's not always an option. More often, clues appear the closer I get. Often a cemetery appears a few miles out.

An Iowa cemetery in a cornfield

Next comes a sign proclaiming, "Litter clean up by the FFA (Future Farmers of America), Honor Society, or 4H Club." Then it's the "Engine Brakes Prohibited" sign, sometimes a "Zoning Permits Required," and finally, a sequence of speed limit signs that progressively drop to 50 mph or 45 mph and in larger towns to 35, and finally 25.

Coon Rapids is a wee bit larger with 1,300 people and a main street with over a dozen occupied storefronts. I stop in the grocery store that makes me feel like I'm back in the 1970s: no neon signs, narrow aisles, definitely not a supermarket. No one rushes, folks are friendly; it feels like what small town America is supposed to be like.

Next, I stop in Manning for a breakfast of eggs, toast, and coffee that sets me back $2, and decide to send more stuff home. I'm still hauling more than I need. First, I need an Allen wrench to take off

BIKING, LESSONS, BLESSINGS AND BEER

my front rack. The front panniers I bought at a neighbor's yard sale are falling apart so I toss them in a trash can. The waitress at the restaurant tells me there's a garage up the road that I ought to visit. I don't think auto mechanics are keen to lending their tools, but this one is. Sure, he'll let me use a wrench. However, after riding for so long, my fingers aren't working too well, and I can't loosen the bolts. The mechanic, with his functioning fingers, happily obliges, and I mail the rack home.

Late that afternoon, I reach Turin and it's all downhill to Onawa, where I plan to camp. There aren't many things more sweeter or rarethan a long steady downhill in the late afternoon. I cruise into town and stop to buy groceries and underwear. Either I lost two pair or accidentally mailed them home. One pair is not enough, and while I've never done it, riding commando intuitively seems like a bad idea. Later I find the other pairs tucked in a side pannier pocket.

I arrive at the Blue Lake KOA campground just before they're closing, at least the office is. The campground is off the main road a ways and there's no one here except a woman working whom I give my $20 fee to pitch a tent and buy a cheap, tall can of Bud. Soon she drives away, and I set up camp. It's quiet, almost deserted, with unoccupied RVs lining the campground's circular road. It's Tuesday and I suppose that folks generally come on weekends and vacations to enjoy the lake. Based on what I've seen, lakes and shade are few and far between out here.

After I cook and eat dinner, I chat with a guy who arrives after me in a classic Airstream RV. He and his wife are taking their granddaughter back to the girl's mother's in Colorado and now there are four of us. A little while later a guy on a motorcycle sets up on the lawn near me and I check him out. I'd like to speak with him, but he doesn't make eye contact. I wonder what he's doing on the road and where he's headed. After his tent's up, he's on the phone for an hour and looks either sad or angry; I can't tell which. I wonder who he's talking to. He's close but not near enough for me to eavesdrop. I can't even hear his voice so he's either mostly listening or talking in hushed tones. Is he talking to his wife, girlfriend, someone else? I can't even create a story in my mind about him. He puts out a weird vibe, or maybe it's just me. I hang out at the picnic table at my site, subtly look in his direction several times, but he still doesn't make eye contact for me to say hi or even nod. It's a little creepy.

The air has gotten thicker and it feels like a storm is imminent, so I stash my bike under a vacant RV. As I lay in my tent, we're hit with powerful wind, rain pounds my tent, and I hear claps of thunder. I stay dry, thankful for my decision to trade the tent for the bivy.

Nebraska

June 28, 2017

Onawa, Iowa to West Point, Nebraska – 50 miles

I wake to a dark, muggy morning. The forecast predicts a short window of dry weather before more storms. I can either ride west 7 miles to Decatur, Nebraska or head back east 4.5 miles to the bigger town of Onawa, get some breakfast, and wait out the storm. Not really much of a choice; I'm going west. I hope I can make it to Decatur before all hell breaks loose. I'll be pissed if I chose poorly.

Before I began this odyssey, I figured Iowa was just a lot of miles to just pass through. How wrong I was. As I near its western border,

I realize how great a time I've had here. It's been my favorite state so far. I cross the underwhelming Missouri River and am welcomed by a billboard, "Nebraska: The Good Life." The good life? I'll be the judge of that soon enough. I look at the signs posted at the entrance to town and think, *this would have been an interesting place for my forbearers.* There's a long list of churches, and a prohibition on peddlers and hawkers. As my childhood next-door neighbor, Betsy, would likely say, "Jewish boys don't bike through Nebraska," a modification of when she saw my snowmobile in Vermont years ago and exclaimed, "Jewish boys don't ride snowmobiles!"

Just up the hill from the Missouri River is the ubiquitous gas station/convenience store. I pull in just before the rain comes. I take this as a good sign and an excellent time to eat breakfast. Alone, facing the unknown with a storm raging outside, I sit down at a table and am joined by Paul. It's amazing how human connection can lighten the mood. Paul is a quite a cool guy who's had an interesting life. When he finds out I'm from Vermont, he tells me about his time in the Navy in the '60s and was stationed in Cape Cod. Maybe to a Nebraskan there's not much difference between Vermont and Massachusetts. Paul once owned the marina on the river, a garage, drove some trucks, but is now mainly retired. We pore over the map and share stories. He has a warm, yet gruff presence, and sharing a breakfast sandwich and coffee makes me feel less alone even though

BIKING, LESSONS, BLESSINGS AND BEER

I'll never see Paul again. I'm learning that it doesn't matter. Paul's here now and we have a stimulating conversation and connection.

Nebraska Paul

At 9 a.m. the rain lets up. The forecast still warns of impending thunderstorms, but if I live by weather forecasts alone, I'd still be in New York. Remember my first night? Zero percent chance of rain. We know how that turned out. Towns in Ohio, Indiana, Illinois, and Iowa are more spread out and have less between them than we do back east, but Nebraska? The map tells me all I need to know. Outside of its eastern cities of Lincoln and Omaha that I plan to avoid, the rest of Cornhusker Country is comprised exclusively of tiny towns with tremendous distances between them.

I stand outside and survey the skies. What will it be, stay dry and comfy in a convenience store, or move on? I hear Meatloaf's signature song in my head, "Paradise by the Dashboard Lights. What's it gonna be boy, yes, or... no?" Might as well get moving.

I think back to the morning before I left home on this trip. I was driving my car near work when I saw two fully loaded bikers ahead of me. I pulled over. On this raw and damp morning, I was very glad to be in my warm, dry car. We were in the middle of a cold, rainy spring, and while training rides were rough, I always headed to the comforts of home afterwards. These two young fellows started in Acadia, Maine and were heading west like I would soon be doing. They were in no rush, weren't covering large swaths of land each day, and I couldn't blame them. I'd be stopping often too to warm up in this weather. I gave them the few Clif bars I had in the car and wished them well. Their route will take them farther north than mine, so I won't see them again.

This interaction gave me pause, but not second thoughts. At the time I thought, what if I have to deal with cold and wet weather day in and day out? I knew it was unlikely with summer coming, and it turned out to be anything but. I head out of Decatur and start climbing away from the Missouri River. I look west and see darkening skies. I am not going back. It doesn't take too many pedal strokes until I'm well outside of town and surrounded by cornfields. Where are the houses, the people, and where is the steeple? It's just me and

BIKING, LESSONS, BLESSINGS AND BEER

the road. I've been told that banks and corporations bought most of the farms and razed the houses. It isn't my imagination; there really aren't many people still living out here.

I hear thunder. There's no place to bailout, no houses nor trees that will provide any sort of protection, not that being under a tree in a thunderstorm makes a lot of a sense. I ride on, spot a house, but as I approach see there's no sign of life. It's the middle of the morning. Are they at work or is the house vacant? I keep going but still don't see a structure in any direction. I continue climbing and the skies ahead are growing darker. Seventeen miles ahead is Bancroft, the next town.

More thunder claps. I'm not worried about getting wet, I'll dry. I am getting nervous about lightning, a leading outdoor killer in the summer. I may not be elevated, but when the only thing around is corn, I feel like there's a bullseye on my back, not to mention that I'm on a metal bike. Being inside a car with rubber tires is supposed to be safe in a lightning storm. Somehow, I doubt the same is true on a bicycle in spite of its two rubber tires. Another burst of thunder, louder and closer. I'm done. There's a house ahead and I don't care if anyone's there. I am finding protection and I'll take my chances, as long as there aren't mean dogs or someone pointing a gun at me. As I near, I see the house is well-kept with a split rail fence surrounding pastures, an intact barn, and black angus cattle out back.

I pull in, lean my bike under the pergola in front of the house, and knock tentatively on the door. An elderly woman answers. Realizing that I must be quite a sight, before she can shut the door I blurt, "Can I sit under your pergola and wait out the storm?" She looks me over and says, "Sure."

A few minutes later she comes back outside and asks, "Would you like something to drink?" I give her my water bottles and she fills them. It's only drizzling but the pergola provides no protection, so I go to the back of the house and stand under the eaves. A few minutes later the woman and her husband come out and ask if I would like to come in. Are they kidding? Next thing I know, I'm seated at their kitchen table, drinking black coffee, and don't care that they don't offer cream coffee or what the weather is doing outside. From the darkness to the light, again.

I spend the next hour in an engaging conversation mainly learning about them. Charlie worked for AT&T for 35 years, they raise black angus, they've got a few children, and they're retired. We talk about the prejudice that exists against Native Americans; I hadn't known how many reservations are here. They say it's the Native Americans who ought to be prejudiced against us—we took their land. We talk about Mexican farm workers and how important they are to the economy here. This is a kind and forward-thinking couple. I like hearing their stories and enjoy their generosity and company.

BIKING, LESSONS, BLESSINGS AND BEER

After the storm blows over, I thank them for their kindness and hospitality and am off into the great unknown.

Shelter from the storm

Although the humidity has eased, the heat has increased, so I stop in Bancroft for a cold drink and shade. I go to my sanctuary, the public library, but it doesn't open for several hours. The town's like the other small towns I pass through, but oddly it's on a steep hill. There are no stores selling food up top, so I head down. I know that I'll have to bike back up, but there aren't any other towns for miles. I coast down the long hill to the only store in town, Ru-De's Mart, the convenience store/gas station. Like the others, this is the town meeting place. Everyone seems to know one another, and I hear talk about the summer recreation program and an upcoming party as I fill my water bottles and Camelback. Rehydrated for now, I bike up the hill, back to Highway 51, now also called S Road, the same road I traveled in from Decatur.

I pedal west on Highway 51 looking for a left turn, which, according to the state map, should be nearby. In a mile, Google Maps tells me to turn left onto 20th Road, the first paved road I come to. In 100 yards the road turns to gravel, harder to ride but not too bad. A few hundred yards later the gravel becomes sand, a whole 'nother story. It can't be too far 'til pavement, I tell myself. After all, Google's bike maps sent me here. The idea of backtracking, especially in this heat and on the sand and gravel, is repugnant. It's 20 miles until the next town, West Point, and already a scorcher at noon.

I opt to keep going south until I turn west onto R Road. It's still sand and I'm putting out a lot of effort, sweating profusely, and barely getting anywhere. I take off my helmet and strap it to the rear rack; it's too damn hot. Just as I think the cycling can't be any worse, I'm looking up a short but steep hill. I start to climb but can't get enough traction, lose my momentum and have to dismount. For the first time on this tour I'm walking. This is the worst.

Eventually the hill levels out and I stay on R Road, sliding in the sand, swerving, concentrating, and trying to keep my bike upright. I'm surrounded by cornfields as far as my eyes can see, not a house, not a car. Corn, only corn.

BIKING, LESSONS, BLESSINGS AND BEER

Like sands through the hourglass, so are the Days of Our Lives

A mile later I come to 22nd Road and turn left, south. Winds blow steadily from the south and gust up to 25 miles per hour. I'm averaging a pitiful 6 miles per hour and manage to accelerate to 11 going downhill all the while under a powerful sun; I am dying.

I intersect Q Road. The map tells me I have to get to the north-south Highway 9 that'll take me into West Point. It should be to my west, and while I don't think it can be that far, I have no idea. I have two choices: I can keep zigzagging to avoid riding directly into the southerly wind or go west until I hit Highway 9.

I decide to to make the next right onto P Road. I crest a smaller hill that I can climb, see a house and trees, and need a rest. When will this end? Even with a vantage point from atop the hill, I can't see pavement among the sea of corn. I make another left, sand, then right, more sand, then left, still sand. This really sucks. I'd jump in the first rig that offers, but the only vehicle I've seen was a truck going the opposite way.

I remind myself that I chose this, biking cross-country, unsupported, making my own route. There's no one out here to help me, give me a ride, or commiserate with. I have no choice but to keep riding. I wanted challenge, an adventure, a goal. Well Amos, how's this working for you? You make your bed, you sleep in it. I keep crawling along and, as was bound to happen eventually, I strike pavement. Black gold. If I weren't so beat, I'd shout with joy. I'll never complain about torn-up, pothole-infested, tar roads after this. And I thought Iowa's gravel stunk.

All in all, it took me an hour and a half to go 9 miles to 17th Road, also known as Highway 9. Nine miles. When I look at the maps later that night, I see that I did pretty much what Google Maps suggested, including the zigzagging. If I had stayed on Highway 51 out of Bancroft for 6 miles instead of making that first left, I would have hit Highway 9 and spent the entire time on pavement. Thanks again, Google.

Even though I'm riding into a stiff and steady wind from the south, drained by the heat and relentless sun, I'm extremely glad to be on pavement. With only 5 miles to go until West Point, I need a break. This is the hottest I've been, and I'm feeling the onset of heat stroke. The only shade is from silos at a grain processing plant, so I

BIKING, LESSONS, BLESSINGS AND BEER

rest there for several minutes along with the scurrying, grain-eating mice.

Nebraska Redwoods

I continue south, extremely slowly, until I reach the intersection of 271 and 9, West Point's city limits. Relief. Then out of nowhere, a biker appears in a University of Nebraska jersey. I'm wearing my Michigan one and he can't believe I'm here; two Big Ten rivals. I think the same thing, and he wants a photo of us together. He's doing a training ride in preparation for a tour over Colorado's four major passes. He wishes me and Michigan well and hopes for better days for the Cornhuskers.

Cornhusker!

It's only 3 p.m. as I enter West Point, Nebraska with its population of 3,364, a veritable metropolis. I am toast. The thermometer outside a motel reads 100 degrees. I've ridden 231 miles in the 2 previous days. That's a lot of time in the saddle, even if there hadn't been as much headwind and heat as there was. While I stayed dry in my tent last night, the thunderstorms made for poor sleeping. I look for both a motel and a place to get a drink. I don't usually stop for the day at 3 in the afternoon, but today is not an ordinary day. It's time to reap the benefits of those century-plus days.

I walk into a convenience store that feels 40 degrees cooler than outside. A group of guys sitting at a booth asks me where I'm going. Up to now, I've been more censored and reserved than I usually am. I'm an East Coaster, after all. I guess my filters are down from the heat and exhaustion because I crack, "To your house for dinner." The

BIKING, LESSONS, BLESSINGS AND BEER

guys laugh. One of the guys, Kevin, who is also the manager, tells me that he's heading out of town in a little while to coach a summer hoops team but wants to treat me to a meal first. Wow. For once in my life my sarcasm actually pays off. Kevin suggests the DQ a mile up the road, so I bike and meet him there. We find a table and he tells me to order what I want. I just get a sandwich, he enjoys an ice cream cone. As Kevin and I sit at a booth, he tells me vignettes about his life, especially his volunteer basketball coaching, which he seems to do a lot of. He shares a sad story about one of his sons who recently died and how his daughter-in-law and grandkids moved here to be closer. He has a gentle way about him that makes me glad I met him.

Kevin's treat at the DQ

After thanking Kevin and bidding him goodbye, I bike back up Lincoln Street (aka Route 275) and roll my bike into the lobby of the first motel I come to, an upscale Super 8. Seriously, it is a good-looking motel. This is another Scott Goodman influence. When he was in college, Scott told me that he brought his bike into classrooms for safe keeping. If students bring their dogs to class, he'd bring his bike. This was the 1970s. While maybe not as bold, I do bring my bike into many places, including motel lobbies. I figure if it's not hurting anything, I'll do it until I'm told not to.

I must've been feeling it after my experience with Kevin because when I approach the woman working behind desk, I say, "I'd like the cross-country biker discount." She's friendly enough, but doesn't respond to my query. As she checks me in and reads my license, Danielle tells me that she's also a Vermonter who moved to Nebraska from Hyde Park, Vermont 3 years ago with some friends. She gives me a discount. I ask her how she likes Nebraska and she tells me, "I like it a lot." Me too. Twice in the course of an hour my humor pays off. From biking on sand through an inferno of corn fields, to meeting three neat folks in West Point. Wonders never cease.

June 29, 2017
West Point to Fullerton, Nebraska – 110 miles

My plan is to make as straight of a line as I could across Nebraska towards the Colorado-Wyoming border where I'll rejoin the TransAmerica route in Walden. With no mountain passes limiting

BIKING, LESSONS, BLESSINGS AND BEER

my options, I have choices. However, after the recent heat and thunderstorms, the distances between Nebraska's towns, and the lack of houses and people make me nervous. Out here, it's field after field of crops, no shade, and at least 25 miles between towns. I reroute my trip towards the Platte River where towns are nearer to one another.

I drag into the town of Albion in the heat of the afternoon. It's been a day of shadeless biking with temps in the 90s taking their toll, and it's time for a cool break. I stop at the Casey's gas station/convenience store, fill my water bottles with Powerade, and ask the two women behind the counter where I can find some great ice cream. "Shorty's!" they exclaim without hesitation.

"It's the best ice cream in town," they tell me with certainty and pride. "You can't miss it. Just go downtown, make a left, and look for the line of people." Obviously, they don't know me. I thank them, mosey downtown and come to not one, but several lefts. Of course, I can miss Shorty's. I can't find it. Again, write down the directions, Amos. I stop two gents outside the bank who tell me that Shorty's is right around the corner.

I get to Shorty's and there's no line, as I'm the only customer for now. I set my bike against a picnic table and walk to the counter to peruse the options. It's a no-brainer, my favorite combo: peanut butter, banana, and hot fudge. I'm proud of myself for at least learning this lesson: *Bike the extra miles for great ice cream.* Of course, I talk with the woman taking my order. She and her mom run Shorty's, named after her grandfather. Soon the mother comes out and the two of them are besides themselves. They cannot believe I've biked from Vermont and am now eating ice cream at their establishment in Albion, Nebraska.

I'm loving my sundae at a picnic table in the shade when a mom and her three little boys sit nearby. They live on a farm outside of town, the kids own bikes, and I tell them about my adventure. It's a treat talking to kids, something I have not had much opportunity to do on this trip.

Albion's best

Shorty's daughter comes over. "Would it be okay if I call the publisher of the local newspaper? I know he'd like to do a story about you."

"Sure," I reply. "How long do you think it will take?" It's getting

BIKING, LESSONS, BLESSINGS AND BEER

late.

"He's right around the corner."

She and her daughter want photos of me and one of me on my bike. I pose for a picture and get a selfie. When my ice cream's finished, I think about ordering another. But it's getting on and the campground is in Fullerton, 25 miles south of here. I ask when the newspaper publisher's coming.

"He's coming," they assure me. I'll wait. Why not? It is kind of neat being a celebrity. The publisher of the Albion Weekly eventually arrives. He and I have a good chat, he takes photos, and I'm on my way. One of the cool things about biking off the established cycling routes is that if people are curious, I'm a novelty and garner positive attention.

I feel good after connecting with folks at Shorty's. I also feel relief from the ice cream and shade, that is, until I resume riding. Unlike the eastern U.S. where late afternoon and early evening mean cooler temperatures, it stays toasty well into the evening in the West.

Never in my life have I paid attention to wind speeds as I do on this trip. Because I'm now zigzagging southwest, I have choices. Westerly winds in the teens are brutal, and after Indiana, I try not to ride when they blow too strongly. It just doesn't seem worthwhile to exert as much energy to go 8 miles per hour when I can go nearly twice as fast without the wind. So today I've paid attention to the weather forecast and choose either south or west, whichever way the wind blows. But now I don't have a choice, I'm heading south to the only campground around and into a fierce headwind. Late, hot, windy. Good times.

Several miles out of Albion, I'm stopped by a ginormous road construction project. I ask the flagger, "Can I ride the shoulder?" She shakes her head no.

"How long's the wait?"

"No hablo inglés," she answers.

"No hay problema," I respond. "Buenas tardes. Hablo español." She smiles and we're off. Meet people where they are. She invites me to share the only shade around, the shadow cast by the adjacent port-o-potty. Being out of the sun and heat is well worth the pungent odor emanating from the portable john. Flagger woman (unfortunately I didn't get her name) tells me both lanes of the highway are closed, and it's not safe to ride ahead. That's fine, I can use the shade and rest. I learn she is Cubana and her husband also works on the crew. She's been in the States for 3 years, doesn't speak English, and isn't planning to learn it. "What happens when this project's over?" I ask. "We move to the next," she answers. Even though she's got a big cooler and sports wide brim hat, I can't help but think how hard and monotonous this work must be. I wait and talk with her for 10 minutes until the pilot car comes. The driver gets out, she changes

BIKING, LESSONS, BLESSINGS AND BEER

places, takes over the wheel, and gives me a signal to follow. Adios, amiga.

La Cubana

I'm in the middle of Nebraska, just me and my bike heading to God-knows-where tonight. I don't know who I'll meet, what the day will bring, and I just had a conversation in Spanish with a Cuban flagger. I love America. I cycle through the massive project and into Fullerton. Riding up the drive to the campground, I'm welcomed to Broken Arrow Wilderness.

This should be interesting and another chance to try something new. I bike down a sandy road past run-down buildings that make me think this was once a church retreat center. It's eerily quiet, a bit creepy, deserted in the the late day shade. I find the office, head in, and am greeted by Doug and his wife. They seem friendly enough but not interested in chit chat or my story. They tell me where I can camp and off I go.

Welcome

I start to unpack and set up camp when Doug comes by in a golf cart. RV parks and golf carts, the new America replacing baseball and apple pie.

"You want to go for a ride on my mule?" he asks.

A mule? I've never ridden a mule. I'm whipped but why not?

Doug heads off to a nearby shed while I wait. I watch him unlock the shed and start a 4x4 vehicle. That's his mule, a Kawasaki Mule, and I thought it was a four-legged hay-burner. He motions to me to hop in.

"Did the sign at the entrance make you want to turn around?" He wants to know as I sit beside him.

"No," I tell him. "There's nothing in it that bothers me." Also, it's not as if I have a lot of choices of places to camp nearby, but I

BIKING, LESSONS, BLESSINGS AND BEER

don't say that out loud. I'm figuring, you only live once.

I don't think Doug gets a lot of company because he sure likes to talk. I enjoy hearing stories, especially since most of the time I'm only talking with myself. Doug takes me up trails so steep and rocky that they'd be challenging to hike. I hold on to the side of the mule as we lean left, then right, and climb almost vertically. Doug has a cowboy hat on his head, I have nothing. I feel the tippiest I've felt on wheels on this trip, even more than sand biking. Any illusion of control is gone; I'm at his mercy. And I'm a tad nervous. I'm in an open 4x4 ascending a grade of at least 25 percent and trusting this yahoo. It's like I'm on a roller coaster with no safety bar, but there's no way I'm going to tell him that I'm afraid or to slow down. I still have some ego. What the hay, when in Nebraska... I'm going to enjoy the trip. Also, I don't get the impression that he wants to die, so let's have fun. I embrace the rocks and turns, figuring Doug must know what he's doing.

When we level out and ride into a clearing, Doug stops and points out sights. He tells me that he has country music concerts at the "park." He also leads hunts.

We get to a knoll where a humongous U.S. flag flies. Then he asks, "What do you think of Trump?"

I debate with myself. Do I tell him how I really feel? Why not? I declare, "Trump's a con man, a huckster, and has no apparent morals."

Doug tells me he is glad Hillary hadn't won. If she had, Doug espouses, he would have had to stop the hunts on his land because she would have stopped gun sales. Huh? I tell him that's what people said for 8 years about Obama. I'm tired of this lie and can't let it go.

"Do you still have your guns?" I ask. Without missing a beat, he counters, "Well, ammo is more expensive." I don't want to get into a political argument with my host and let it drop.

We ride to a meadow with an expansive view. Doug continues guiding. He asks if I've seen the movie, "Dances with Wolves". I have, several times. He tells me the movie's story is based on events that happened here. One name for the facing cliff is "Buffalo Leap" because Native Americans used to drive small herds of buffalo off of it. Seems reasonable.

After we descend, Doug drops me back at my tent site. That was cool; Doug didn't have to take me for that ride. I'm again the recipient of kindness and generosity from strangers, especially those who seem so different from me.

Back at the "campground" I explore and discover there aren't any amenities. There's one other camper in a small RV, and the only bathroom is quite a ways, so I use the trees instead. I swim in the delightfully refreshing Cedar River, much better than a shower. There's no beach as it appears recent storms washed away a lot of shoreline and knocked down a mess of trees. Doug is bucking some

BIKING, LESSONS, BLESSINGS AND BEER

up as I swim. I think of the welcome sign and another lesson learned.

A warning tells you to pay attention. It's not a prohibition nor even a suggestion.

June 30, 2017

Fullerton to Kearney, Nebraska – 105 miles

Since there's no one around for me to join in the Lord's Prayer, no country music playing, and no one shooting guns, I rise early, pack, and head out. I bike to my friendly, neighborhood Casey convenience store for coffee. People come in and out, heading to work I assume, but not me. I sit down and am joined for breakfast by Laverne, a sweet Nebraska native. He's older, soft spoken, slow moving. We talk about Nebraska and ourselves. Ah, the humanity I encounter on this voyage.

After a few hours of nondescript cycling through Nebraska farmland, I'm in the town of Wolbach which dictates my stop as much as anything else. I've established a loose goal of biking 50 miles before noon each day. Mornings are the best times to ride, both energy- and weather-wise. Riding another 50-plus miles in the afternoon and early evening usually isn't too hard if the wind is gentle. Regardless of where I am, when I started, or what the weather conditions are, by the end of the day I've averaged 10 miles per hour. If I begin cycling at 6:30 a.m. and end 11 hours later at 5:30 p.m., I've gone 110 miles. Start at 7 and end at 5, 10 hours and 100 miles. Have a headwind, hills, long stops, short rests, 10 mph. On afternoons when I have a tailwind I often push farther. I do have a vague idea of where I may end up each night, but the 10 mile per hour rate is uncanny.

Laverne

Wolbach, Nebraska, population 259, has the same look and feel of most of the midwest towns I've passed through: a post office, a bank, a library, a bar, sometimes a still operating school or grocery store, empty storefronts, and few people milling about. Buildings in these towns look like they haven't been painted or repaired in decades. I don't find anything calling to me on Main Street, but when I reach the end of the block heading out of town, I spot R & R Pump, a gas station that is anything but a convenience store.

BIKING, LESSONS, BLESSINGS AND BEER

Definitely not a convenience store

Since the next town is 20 miles away, I'm going in. As soon as I enter, I know I made the right choice. This is how I remember gas stations, the gas stations of my youth, before they became fluorescent-lit, corporate clones. There's no coffee bar, no slurpee machine, no soda fountain, and no pizza or hot dogs underneath heat lamps. A high school girl is working behind the counter where fresh eggs are for sale. Shelves are stocked with motor oil and auto supplies, and a single coffee pot sits on a table along with one-size styrofoam cups. There's a room out back whose walls are stocked with boxes and cans of food. Seated around a big table in the center of the room is a group of old-timers.

I head over to the coffee pot, drop a quarter in a cup, and take a styrofoam cup while one of the old timers comes up behind me. There's only a cup's worth left in the pot, so I motion for him to take it. "It's for you," he says. I empty the pot as one of the other old-timers comes over from the table. He asks for a cup, the guy behind me laughs and calls out, "No more. You have to make a new pot."

I take my coffee to the back room. The fellas make a spot for me and continue their banter. They are ripping on each other. Imagine you're 75 years old, hanging with your boyhood friends, and drinking your daily coffee with the same guys you've known your whole lives. It's like the social hierarchy hasn't changed since junior high.

They're still cutting up, cracking on one another, laughing. They're not mean, not showing off, just having a good time at one another's expense.

I ask what they do or did, and they tell me who used to farm when he wasn't in Florida, who pretended to be a mechanic, and who drove a truck. One of them is clearly the sharpest and one seems to be kind of slow, and it's if they've welcomed me to their lunch table in the school cafeteria. Moments like these in Wolbach, Nebraska, so far in more than just miles from Norwich, Vermont, that continue to warm my spirit.

Sharing coffee can do that. Once, in the early morning I was walking through the cloistered streets in Stonetown, Zanzibar when a group of head-covered, Muslim men invited me to enjoy their Turkish coffee. We can't talk to one another using words but do so using body and sign language. I'm heartened by their welcome and

BIKING, LESSONS, BLESSINGS AND BEER

the coffee was superb, dark, and strong. This was not long after 9/11, in the same city where I saw street vendors hawking t-shirts with Osama Bin Laden's portrait.

There's never a perfect time to leave. I don't want to overstay my welcome and always want to ride in the cooler, less windy mornings, but I sure like hanging out with these old-timers. After good laughs and two small cups of coffee, it feels like it's time to continue towards the Platte.

Being on my bike, I don't stop at many museums and tourist attractions, mainly because all I have is connected to my bicycle. I only part with my bike when I go into a store, park where I can see my bike at a restaurant or have a place to safely store it like a motel or a home. Today I'm passing through St. Paul and I see that the Museum of Nebraska Major League Baseball is here. I figure it's worth a stop. First, I get a snack at a Casey's convenience store. As I unlock my bike, a young guy comes over, and asks what I'm doing. After I tell him he grins and shakes his head in amazement. He wants to shake my hand. Of course.

I bike a few blocks to the museum which is within the St. Paul Area Chamber of Commerce and the Howard County Visitor Center. It's just me and the woman who works here. The museum features photos and memorabilia of Cornhusker players, dominated by hometown pitching legend Grover Cleveland, as well as Wade Boggs and former Met, Richie Ashburn. It's a unique American treasure, a mini Cooperstown, and I'm glad I made the stop.

Worth the visit

Leaving town on a quiet side street, a car pulls next to me, windows down. This may sound unsettling, but I've yet to feel threatened or intimidated by another human being on the entire voyage. The man driving asks about my trip, and when I tell him, he gets out of his car and asks if he can shake my hand. Twice in one day, in one town. *Share the joy.* Seems like Nebraskans get a charge out of long-distance cyclists.

I continue on, enjoying the fact that I have absolutely no idea what the day will bring. This is the case every single day, but now every place and person are new to me. Rarely does a day go by when biking isn't bookended by something exceptional, challenging, and most often both. Unlike my daily routines back home, I'm experiencing new places and new people non-stop, often counting on

BIKING, LESSONS, BLESSINGS AND BEER

the goodness of strangers and feeling a heightened sense of being alive.

As I weave south and west toward the Platte River, the skies become cloudier and the cool temperature's a welcome change. I reach the intersection in Cairo and have a choice to make: go straight or turn right? Straight is south, right leads west, both eventually will lead me towards Kearney, a good-sized city on the Platte River. Since I have neither a fixed immediate destination nor a bike route to follow, I consult the state bicycle map.

The Nebraska State Bike Map is a color coded. Each state highway line has a color corresponding to the average number of vehicles that travel along it each day. So far, I have done quite well, aside from my sand roads fiascos that aren't even on the map. The road west from Cairo to Ravenna is purple. Purple is good, the next to least traveled road of the four vehicle density levels, so west towards Ravenna it is. I head out of Cairo on a wide, paved shoulder along with plenty of cars and RVs. It's the start of the 4th of July weekend, and Ravenna is on the way to lakes and recreation areas. I figure it'll be fine for the hour I have to ride on this road until... the shoulder turns to sand. Sand. Freakin' Nebraska. Maybe the sand will be short-lived.

I keep riding (what choice do I have?), concentrating on keeping my front wheel straight and not skidding. This isn't the beach-like stretch between Bancroft and West Point where I had the road to myself. Skidding and sliding were a royal pain but not a matter of life or death. Now I'm on a crazy, busy highway alongside cars and campers zipping by at 65 miles per hour. I'm scared. Two miles of painfully slow, nerve-racking riding later and I'm still on sand. I've ridden 5 miles from Cairo and have 12 more miles until I reach Ravenna. I'm in no man's land; nothing around but this highway. At this rate 12 miles will take me 2 hours riding in highly anxious state the whole time. In hindsight, I suppose I could have turned around and gone back the 2 miles on sand, but that doesn't even cross my mind. It never does. I keep hoping that the sand will end just ahead. It does not.

Riding a sandy shoulder is insane; there's no other way to describe it. When this happened in Pella, Iowa, I got off the highway as soon as I could. Here I don't see a way out. Cars, pickups, RVs zoom by and I keep riding, slowly, cautiously. Eventually I see a turn up ahead on my left, south. I can go south instead of west, so waiting for a break in the traffic, I run my bike across the highway. Yee ha! The road's paved. I'm not sure where this goes, but anywhere is better than the sand shoulder. I celebrate too soon because I'm back on sandy dirt. With no idea where this road will take me, I pedal back to the highway, seriously discouraged.

All the while the sky's getting darker, and at some point this afternoon, all hell will let loose. If I were anxious before, now I'm as nervous as I've been on this trip. I just don't see any way out. Up ahead is a large, wooden road sign welcoming travelers to the Ravenna Recreation Region. Hmmm. I stop, lean my bike against the sign, take off my helmet, and stick out my thumb. I did a lot of hitchhiking in my younger days, but never with a bike. All I need right now is one ride, one pickup truck, and I'll be saved. I stand with my thumb out trying to look respectable, whatever that means. Fifteen minutes pass, nada. No one even slows down. Nobody hitches anymore. I can wait here all day, not get a ride, get soaked, and not be any closer to where I'm heading. I get back on the bike. I've gone 7 miles, 10 left until I get to Ravenna. At the rate I'm going it'll be another hour of terror. As if it can't get worse, the sky ahead is turning darker still and the air is palpably heavier. I'm heading directly into a storm.

I pedal ever so slowly and cautiously until the shoulder turns to gravel. This is a huge improvement over sand and my apprehension is somewhat allayed. However, the sky is even darker. Adrenaline shoots through my body, propelling me to churn faster now that I'm able to ride more confidently on the gravel. The last thing I need is to be riding in a rainstorm with cars zooming by not being able to see me. As I close in on Ravenna, the shoulder improves. I bike harder, frequently looking at my odometer. Four miles to go. I'm going 15 miles per hour, I can be there in 15 minutes. Three miles to go. At this pace I'll be there in just over 10 minutes. I feel the air getting thicker. I pedal hard, really moving. Two miles to go and I feel drops. There's no shelter in sight so I keep hammering. I figure the rain is more of a nuisance than safety at this point. How little I know about Nebraska.

It starts raining harder. I spot a veterinary office across the street and go for it. It's closed, the adjacent garage is locked, and the roof overhang does not provide much shelter. I get back on the bike, hightail it, and soon spot a gas station ahead. I sprint and try to find a place to protect my bike. It's raining for real now, so I wheel my bike into the gas station. The young woman at the counter says it is okay for me to bring my bike into the attached tire shop. I do, buy a cheese popper from the warmer and then, boom! My first midwest hailstorm. Holy cow. Marble-sized pellets bounce off the parking lot and picnic table. I made it just in the nick of time. I could have been riding on the highway with hail balls bouncing off my helmet.

I'm spent. The last few hours of fear and adrenaline sapped my energy. I'm eager to have a quiet break, charge my phone, and wait out the storm in the tire shop. Someday I may learn not to have expectations. Today is not that day. Usually my open vibe has brought good tidings, so when the tire shop owner decides to engage me in conversation, I'm glad to oblige. His discourse quickly turns to politics, specifically Trump.

"What do you think of him?" he wants to know. Hmmm... Do

BIKING, LESSONS, BLESSINGS AND BEER

I want to go there? Something about the way he asks makes me think that Tire Guy voted for him and he's setting me up for debate. I have no interest in changing his mind, and except for the campground owner last night, have purposefully avoided talking politics with strangers. I'm a guest in his store, but he asked, so it would be rude not to answer, wouldn't it? I suppose I could have said, "I don't pay attention to politics," but it's hard for me to lie. And it's hard for me to shut up even though I have become a much better listener on this trip. I could have told him, "I don't like to talk politics," but that's not really true either. So, I turn the question on him.

"What do you think about him?"

"I voted for Trump mainly because Trump isn't Hillary and he won't continue the 'failed' policies of Obama. Obama ruined the economy. Obama was pro-gay and pro-transgender and this is leading to our country's demise."

"Who did you want to be president?" I ask.

"I wanted Ted Cruz. Hillary lost," he tells me, "because the Democrats didn't pay attention to the evangelicals." He may be correct.

"Okay," I say. "You might be right. But Trump? He's not a conservative and he's sure not a practicing Christian." Tire Guy doesn't disagree but he's adamant that Trump is better than Hillary. He thinks the problem is Washington in general. Tire Guy is coherent, so I ask him,

"What would you do to fix things there?"

"I'd go to Washington," he tells me, "and into Congress. I'd ask each Congressman, 'Mr. Congressman, do you know the ten commandments?' Then I'd have him recite them. We're a Christian country founded on Judeo-Christian values," he continues. This is his plan?

"What about the 1st amendment?" I ask. "The separation of church and state. What about Buddhists, Hindus, and atheists?"

He doesn't answer. By this time the rain and hail have stopped, and I take this as a sign that it's time to go. I thank him for the conversation and letting me stay in his shop. I mean it. I learned a lot about how another person sees the world while my bike and I stayed dry. I don't care if I changed his mind and sure hope we are not a country full of people who think like him. But he was kind enough to let me stay in his shop, and he certainly entertained me.

I'm only 30 miles from Kearney, giving me I enough time to make it there by evening, even with the Siren song getting louder. It's going to be a 100-plus mile day, including some of the most harrowing riding thus far, not to mention a hail storm. I'll be looking for a motel tonight. As I ride as far to the right of a shoulder-less road that I can, a driver yells at me for biking on the road. Does he expect me to bike off the road? This is the first time this has happened since I was

BIKING, LESSONS, BLESSINGS AND BEER

flipped off on day one.

Kearney is by far the biggest city I've biked in since Buffalo, and what I see of it on this Friday evening consists of nasty miles riding along strip malls, fast food joints, and finally, motels. There's no shoulder, so I alternate between riding on the crappy sidewalks and the right lane, eventually choosing the lane instead of the sidewalk. I'm in no mood to mess around, cars be damned.

I check into a motel and am psyched for dinner at the Mexican restaurant across the street. When I get there, I see the "Closed" sign in the window. Dang. I meander down the road, exhausted, walking slowly, and feeling hangry. I don't want to go to the Perkins family restaurant next door and then I spot Kings Buffet. Perfect!

The Chinese restaurant lives up to its name. I have my own booth and fill a plate with broccoli, snow peas, baby corn, and more veggies. So good. That finished, I get another plate, this time General Tsao's chicken. I finish the chicken then chow on shrimp with garlic sauce. More veggies? Absolutely. How about a plate of Shanghai stir-fry noodles? Next, fried tofu, a little wonton soup, and for the grand finish: a dessert of cookies and ice cream. All for one price, $11. I think the food even tasted good. Another silver lining at the end of a rough day.

July 1, 2017

Kearney to North Platte, Nebraska – 102 miles

Today I'll parallel the Platte River and return to the same Lincoln Highway to which I was briefly introduced when I crossed into Indiana. The Lincoln Highway runs coast-to-coast from Times Square to San Francisco. It was America's first national memorial to President Abraham Lincoln and one of our first transcontinental highways. Running adjacent to the railroad and the river and usually out of sight of I-80, it's a mighty fine bike route with wide shoulders and minimal traffic. The Nebraska State Bike Map, which I now pay closer attention to, shows that it's densely traveled around Kearney, so I'll try to join it outside the city limits.

Since I paid for it, I have coffee and cereal at the motel and leave at 6:30 a.m. The map makes it look like I can cross the Platte River and I-80 and take back roads west while keeping the river to my north. The sun's my best compass to make sure I'm going west. As long as I stay on pavement and avoid sand roads and dead ends, what can go wrong?

It's a gorgeous early morning, my favorite time to ride, cool and quiet. There's no traffic heading out of the city on a Saturday morning at this hour and after crossing I-80, I'm on beautiful, placid, and flat

BIKING, LESSONS, BLESSINGS AND BEER

county roads. I watch deer in the cornfields, a fox trot, and hawks soar overhead. It's too early for heat or wind, just perfect riding and I enjoy 10 fun miles of cycling. This route takes me a little out of the way but it's well worth it. *Choose beauty over speed.* I know I'll have to get on the Lincoln Highway sooner or later as these back roads will turn to dirt or end. When and where are the looming questions.

I follow the small lines on the map until I think I'm nearing the end of my peaceful easy feeling. When I'm driving, I'm reluctant to ask for directions. Not exactly sure where I am? Step on the gas and go. Lost while biking can mean lots of extra pedaling. I see a house on my right with the garage doors open, so I stop. I ask the man working on a sawhorse about the road ahead. He lets me know that I need to make the next turn. Perfect timing.

Ask for directions. It's only taken me three plus weeks to maybe figure this out. Maybe you can teach an old dog new tricks.

We talk, his wife comes out, and the smiling couple offer me a seat and a cold Gatorade. I really should ask for directions more often.

A delightful break outside Kearney

There will be no sand for me today. Coming down to the Platte and the Lincoln ighway is one of the wisest decisions I make. Because it parallels I-80 and the Platte River, small towns crop up every 10 to 15 miles instead of the 30 to 50 miles had I gone due west. The extra miles of riding are well worth the comfort and peace of mind. Plus, on my left are miles-long freight trains to gaze at.

I bike for a spell without coming across much of anything, just the no man's land between highways and an occasional house, when I see an open store. It's a fishing tackle and bait store that also sells mugs and posters that proclaim, "Give a man a fish and he'll eat for a day... or teach a man to fish and get rid of him on weekends!" "Everyone needs to believe in something... I believe I'll go fishing." "I'm 64 and my rod still works." The shop is strictly old school, the

BIKING, LESSONS, BLESSINGS AND BEER

anti-Cabelas. Rows are tightly packed and narrow; posters and paintings adorn every possible space. Since I'm not searching for souvenirs to add to my panniers, I'm happy to see there's a cooler. I buy a powerade and ask the owner if he has coffee. He brews a fresh pot, but he's not talkative so I drink most of the cream-less coffee quickly and hit the road.

At Lexington, I veer off the Lincoln Highway for my next break as it appears that there's a town with more than a convenience store, and I want a snack. I make a right turn down Main Street and enter another world. Men and women are dressed in traditional African clothing, store signs are in Spanish, I see women in hijabs. Where am I? I thought I was in the middle of Nebraska. Turns out that Lexington is home to a Tyson meat packing plant and the city is full of recent immigrants. Who else would do this work?

When I get to the outer edge of downtown, I spot the Panaderia, Nuevo Amanacer. Excellent. I love the opportunity to converse in Spanish. I enter, am the only customer, and I start speaking Spanish with the woman behind the counter. She asks what I'm doing in Lincoln, and when I tell her, she insists I bring my bike into the bakery for safe keeping. She takes me in the backroom where her husband's baking. She's Mexican-American from California and he's from Mexico. They're gracious and their sunny dispositions make me feel welcome. I enjoy a yummy cuernito and coffee and chillax for a half-hour. When I go up to the register to pay, I'm greeted by a middle-aged Anglo. He tells me he's the owner and undercharges me, intentionally, I think.

A taste of Mexico in Lexington

The temperature's in the 80s and with all sun all afternoon, the decision to ride along the Platte River continues to reap benefits. It would've been brutal cycling across the middle of Nebraska with neither towns nor shade. Instead, every hour or so I stop at a convenience store for ice water, or Powerade, iced tea, lemonade, shade, and air conditioning. Who'd have imagined that convenience stores can be sanctuaries?

As I bike along the lightly traveled Route 30, a car slows and pulls next to me with its windows down. Again. Only in Nebraska.

BIKING, LESSONS, BLESSINGS AND BEER

Sounds freaky but it doesn't feel this way in the least. Maybe it's because I'm in the middle of Nebraska or maybe it's because it is the middle of the day. It could be because that's where my head is, open and trusting. Moreover, the guy driving looks okay and as he drives alongside me, he starts asking about my trip. He tells me that he lives in Alaska and is planning a big bike trip there.

After realizing that we can't very well have a conversation with him driving next to me, he pulls ahead and stops. He gets out of his car and it's obvious that he really wants to talk, so I get off my bike.

"I'm Greg," he shakes my hand.

"Amos."

"Where you headed today?" he asks. I begin to tell him and then say,

"I would love to talk more but standing here in the blazing sun is rough. Do you want to meet me at the next convenience store?"

"Tell you what," he answers. "I'm heading to Brady, about 30 miles west. We're having a family reunion. Why don't you stop by? I'm not sure we can put you up but there's lots going on. It's at the town building. Murphy Family Reunion. Hard to miss."

"Sounds good. I'll see you there," I answer and think: *This ought to be something.*

Greg drives ahead and I bike on, stopping one more time at another convenience store for a drink. When I reach Brady, I stop at the town store to find out where the town building is. I hear folks talking about the steam engine heading our way. Apparently every once in a great while a refurbished old steam engine drives down the tracks, supposedly something to see. I head back to the railroad tracks, approach a couple sitting in a pick-up truck and ask about the locomotive. Jackpot.

Not only are they waiting for the steam engine, but the driver of the pick-up is a freight train engineer who's been driving locomotives right here on the Platte for 30 years. I pepper him with questions, and he provides me quite a lesson. The North Platte Rail Yard is the largest in the world with some of the freight trains extending for 3 miles; that's why they need several locomotives to pull them. When the trains are headed east, they usually bring containers and goods from the Pacific, going west they tend to be empty. The couple has a rough idea about when the train will arrive, but it's getting late and I want to meet Greg. I thank them for their time and knowledge, cross the road, and start down one of Brady's handful of streets. With 400 people living in town, it can't be that hard to find the community center. I don't have to look long because who should come driving towards me in the other direction but Greg. It's been a few hours since we parted, and he's on his way back up the Lincoln Highway to see if I'm okay.

I follow Greg to the town building where the front is adorned

BIKING, LESSONS, BLESSINGS AND BEER

with a "Murphy Reunion" banner, signs, and balloons. Greg and I head inside where some family members mill around inside while most are visiting the family cemetery. I arrive too late to play games and eat lunch with them, but they've got lots of food left and several women insist I eat. They don't have to ask me twice. Fried chicken, salad, cookies, they even give me some for the road. I'm treated like an honored guest. Greg's grandparents used to live in Brady and the cousins spent summers here as children. They hold this reunion every 4 years and family come from all over the country.

Greg is a mensch and I feel an easy connection with him. He currently teaches P.E. part-time in Alaska and runs basketball clinics for kids with special needs around the world. I find this cool, but what Greg tells me next blows me away. For 20 years Greg was an assistant coach with the New York Knicks, my boyhood team who practiced in a college gym that I played in as a kid. I was an adult when Greg worked with the Knicks, but I watched the guys he coached. They had some good teams in those days, perennially in the playoffs, but lost in the 1995 semis to Indiana when Patrick Ewing missed a sure-thing finger roll at the buzzer. As if to prove it, Greg calls Patrick Ewing while we sit at the table and wishes "Pat" a happy July Fourth.

It's a beautiful respite and I become an honorary member of the Murphy clan, Amos Murphy. I could stay but I have a Warm Showers tomorrow in Ogallala and have miles to cover if I'm going to make it.

I haven't had a homestay for some time and there aren't any others until I get to Fort Collins. I bid the Murphys thanks and goodbye and head west.

There are two camping options in North Platte, 25 miles from Brady. Cody Park is smack dab in the city, and Buffalo Bill State Recreation Area is a ways out. Every other time in my life I would have chosen the more rustic state park. Alone and on my bike, I opt for urban camping. Heck, it's Nebraska. I arrive at Cody Park late in the afternoon and find the grass patch on the side of the road that's the designated camping site. I walk to the municipal pool, but it just closed. Too bad, a dip would have been delightful. But the kiddie amusement park next door with its mini rides, carousel, concession stand, and ice cream is open and rocking. I watch families play while I eat ice cream.

There's also tennis, disc golf, softball, horseshoes, an historic train display, a picnic area, and an animal enclosure with deer, elk, burros, sheep, peafowl, ducks, and geese. I've never camped in a place like this. There are only several occupied sites and a family with a few small kids are the only ones I make contact with. It's always a different vibe in the city. I lock my bike to the picnic table and chow on more Murphy family fried chicken before calling it a night.

BIKING, LESSONS, BLESSINGS AND BEER

July 2, 2017

North Platte to Ogallala, Nebraska – 53 miles

Riding along the Platte is the same today: flat, not scenic, and freight trains are enterntaining for only so long. I'm looking forward to a change. Half-way to Ogallala, I stop at the Paxton Pit Stop, a non-chain, non-convenience store gas station and grocery and I'm in for something different. I buy a bag of Nebraska popcorn and sit in one of the two booths. Papers are scattered about, and I try to clean the salt I've spilled. I'm just glad to be out of the sun for a bit. The store's empty except for me and Dennis, the owner, who's in the booth behind me. He soon comes over to my booth and takes a seat across from me. We exchange greetings and I notice the "For Sale" sign in the window.

You're selling this? I ask him.

"Trying to. Been here a long time."

"What are your plans?"

"I've got a motorcycle and me and my wife want to tour more."

Across the street from us is Ole's Big Game Steakhouse. It looks interesting with antlers adorning the wooden entrance.

"Is it any good?" I ask, pointing to the restaurant.

"No," he tells me, nodding to Ole's. "Not anymore. The Lounge and Windy Gap Bar and Saloon, (also visible) is much better."

Dennis the raconteur

Dennis starts telling me about a fight between some cheating spouses that happened at the saloon. It cascaded into the street and sounds like something out of the wild west, people and furniture flying. Dennis is quite a character and storyteller. Then he begins the most bizarre story that has a distant connection to Ole's and the fight. I've met some raconteurs on this trip, but he takes the cake.

"One day," he starts, "this woman comes in. She's riding a motorcycle, so I immediately like her. Now she's also a good-looking lady. Real fine. She tells me she's a documentary filmmaker and asks me if there are any characters in town. Right away I tell her about Jimmy, the guy who started the bar fight at Ole's. 'He'll be great,' she

BIKING, LESSONS, BLESSINGS AND BEER

says. Jimmy lives outside town. I give her directions and off she goes.

"Well the next day, Jimmy comes in. The woman went to his house and brought her video equipment inside. She makes him sign a disclosure. Then they have wild sex. She does things to him..."

By this time, I don't know what's what. What is happening on the Platte River? First, I bike into the multi-cultural world of Lexington, then I'm part of a family reunion, I camp next to an amusement park and zoo, and now I'm told an X-rated tale. Who thinks Nebraska's dull? Dennis wraps up his tale, I thank him for the stories, and am off to Ogallala. I'm a tourist in my own country.

Back on the Lincoln Highway with its wide shoulders and ample room to bike to the right of the rumble strips. For me, rumble strips offer an illusion of safety, a wake-up call for drivers but no sort of barrier that will stop the hunks of steel to my left. Still, I feel safer with them than without.

For the past 2 days I've been texting with Jo, my host in Ogallala. Jo tells me that she and her family are heading out on their boat this afternoon; I'm welcome to join them or stay and chill at their home. I'm not much of a motorboat aficionado and consider the possibility of just hanging in a house to myself, but, when in Nebraska... Besides, it's 90 degrees, I have plenty of alone time, and boating on a lake seems like a cool way to hang with new folks.

Riding conditions are perfect, and I tell Jo I'll be there by early afternoon. She gives me her address and tells me where the key is in case they've left before I get there. I end up arriving while they're still home and wouldn't be chilling had I stayed back. Their air conditioner's on the fritz. Their high school son Dan, husband Ted, Jo, and I pack the truck with food and drink, hitch up the boat, and the four of us plus dog head to the lake.

I'm immediately made to feel welcome as they tell me their story. They moved here from Wyoming a few years ago for Ted's job, the same one from which he was recently laid off. Now he's back working in Wyoming, coming home for weekends, their house is for sale and soon they'll all move back to Wyoming. A daughter works as a geologist for an oil company, a son attends the University of Wyoming, and Dan is headed there in the fall. After the boat ride Ted's heading back to Wyoming, about 4 hours from Ogallala. With all this going on in their lives, they still make the effort and take the time to host me. They're not even bikers. A few years ago, Ted was driving in Wyoming and encountered a group of four German cyclists caught in a snowstorm. Ted invited them to their house and a Warm Showers host family was born.

After driving 30 minutes through the prairie, we arrive at Lake McConaughy. It is mind-blowing. The gigantic reservoir covers 55 square miles, has over 100 miles of shoreline, is over 140 feet deep and looks other-worldly. A giant body of water spreading out in a desert

BIKING, LESSONS, BLESSINGS AND BEER

tableau created by damming the Platte River.

We load the boat with gear, hop in, and we're off on a tour of the lake. As we motor, we pass several tent cities with hundreds, maybe even thousands of people on each of the shorelines that have beaches and road access. Who can blame them? A body of water in this heat? In spite of the masses on scattered shorelines, life on the water is calm and quiet except when Dan guns the motor. Ninety degrees doesn't feel too toasty when you're zipping along at 40 miles per hour. We stop to swim in comfortably cool water and chat with a pair of boys spearfishing. Dan and Ted used to spearfish and share pointers with the young fishermen. I enjoy my first two Leinenkugel's Summer Shandies, dee-licious. This motorboating ain't half-bad.

Later in the afternoon the clouds start stacking. A serious storm's brewing so we pack up and head home. There's a flurry of activity as Dan tries in vain to fix the A/C, we eat a smorgasbord of home cooking, watch the Cardinals win, and Ted packs and leaves for Wyoming. Then the sky becomes pitch black and the winds whip something fierce. We close all the doors and windows. Am I about to experience my first tornado? It turns out to be only a monster thunderstorm. After it lets up, Jo and I make a trip to the Safeway so I can stock up on food for tomorrow's long trek across the desolate prairie and into Colorado.

Colorado

July 3, 2017

Ogallala, Nebraska to Sterling, Colorado – 98 miles

I wake up early anticipating a tough day, 90 mostly barren, hot miles to Sterling, Colorado. I bought plenty of food last night since without cycling maps, I'm not confident I'll pass anything resembling a grocery store on this stretch. I pack my things in Jo and Ted's garage, and for some reason, think I should check my handlebar bag for my credit card, ATM card, driver's license, and the $40 I have rubber-banded together. That and my passport (for the short jaunt into Canada) are all I'm carrying, no wallet. My cards aren't in the bag. Odd. I'm pretty good about keeping them in the same spot. Then

BIKING, LESSONS, BLESSINGS AND BEER

I remember last night for the grocery trip I put the cards in my pocket since I was driving with Jo and didn't bring the handlebar bag. Hmmm. They must have fallen out of my pocket.

I search the bedroom. Nothing. I go through the kitchen, my panniers, bike shorts, bathroom. Not there. I search the same places again. I still can't find them. This is not good. I take deep breaths as panic starts to creep in.

I Google directions to the Safeway supermarket where Jo and I went late last night. I paid with my credit card, so I know I had my cards then. Maybe I hadn't tucked them deep enough into my pocket and they fell out in the parking lot. If I get there now, just after dawn, they may still be laying there. I sprint over, blowing through stop signs.

I scour the parking lot. Nothing. It's 6:15 a.m. and the front doors to the Safeway are locked. I pry them open, trying not to look as hysterical as I'm beginning to feel. If someone had found my credit card last night and used it, that would not be good. If no one had found it, then what?

The store's empty. I hustle to the office and before the manager can kick me out, start explaining why I'm here. She's sympathetic and looks in the office to see if anyone turned in my things. No luck. Then she opens the register I used last night it, looks in it and under the drawer. Nothing. Damn, this is not good. I'm in western Nebraska with no money. On the other hand, I do have food and a tent.

I bike back to Jo's unsure of my next move. What to do? I search the house again, the third time. Nothing. I better cancel my credit card, so I call Visa. I'm not sure about a replacement card. Where would I have it sent?

Jo's now up and and as I fill her in on the morning events, she wants to know how she can help. I tell her that she already has by hosting me, extremely graciously at that. Also, there's really nothing she can do. Jo tells me she'll check with the police to see if the credit card turns up and we'll talk later.

So much for the early start. I say goodbye to Jo, thank her, she gives me a hug, and I head towards Colorado. I've had a really great time in Nebraska, much more so than I ever could have dreamed. Up 'til now I thought biking across the middle of the country would be extremely dull. Boy was I wrong. I loved the plains and had phenomenal experiences with fantastic folks. Colorado will mark another state and another region, the beginning of the Rockies, even if I am busted.

According to the state map, leaving Ogallala is straightforward. Stay on Route 30 for a few miles and make the first left. When I come to the first left, I turn onto hard pack. Then it becomes sand. You've got to be friggin' kidding me. As if this morning can't get any worse. I love Nebraska, but this sand is killing me. Again, with the sliding, the fighting to stay upright, and the glacial pace that's not much faster than walking. Luckily only one truck passes and a half-hour later I find myself in a paved high school parking lot in Brule, NE, population 300. I get water at the gas station, and the guy working there tells me that I turned too soon. If I stayed on Route 30 until the next paved left, I would have avoided the sand. Again. He can't believe I just biked that section because it isn't done. Well it is now. Boy do I miss the bike maps.

After 20 miles of riding through the lifeless, barren, countryside, I'm greeted by a "Welcome to Colorful Colorado" sign. Bull. Aside from the grass and trees near the sign, the landscape is brown as far as the eye can see, including the welcome sign itself. I am not in a great mood. Actually, I'm quite pissy after losing my access to money and landing in another sand trap. Thirty-one miles from Ogallala, I stop in the first town I come to with more than a gas station, Julesburg, Colorado. It's late morning and getting hot so I take a break in the shade between a few buildings. Suddenly I've got it. I'm not sure why I didn't think of this earlier. I'll find a bank and get money wired to me. Problem solved.

Excited, I get on my bike and ride down Julesburg's main street. I see a small bank, Co-Ne Federal Credit Union. I enter and tell the first person who asks me, "How may I help you?" my predicament. They don't do money transfers, of course, but she tells me there's a bigger bank around the corner that should be able to help.

I head down the block feeling optimistic and lock my bicycle outside the Point West Community Bank. I tell the first representative my situation. Because I'm not a customer they won't help me. Screw it. I don't have the gumption to fight or plead. I still have 40 miles of nothingness to ride through, it's only getting hotter, and I have plenty of food. I need to ride, not beg or argue, and certainly not worry.

Fifteen miles later I reach Sedgwick with few signs of its 149 residents. There's a town office building that's actually open with people working and they allow me to use their bathroom. Afterwards, I walk down the street to the nearly empty Sedgwick Cafe where the two women working/chatting there say I can fill my bottles with ice water. I'm the only "customer" and even though I'd like to, I can't afford to buy anything. I don't have the money.

Then it's back on Route 138 through the prairie. It's hard to imagine if you've not experienced this, but there really is nothing between these towns. Plains after plains with no signs of human existence except the mostly deserted road, fencing, and some old oil wells. This is the first time I truly experience the tremendous vastness of the land, just how small I am, and I'm beginning to feel a tad vulnerable. I felt something similar when facing thunderstorms in Nebraska, nervous about what might come, but this is different.

BIKING, LESSONS, BLESSINGS AND BEER

There is literally is nothing around for miles. I know that I have camping gear and food, but I have the sensation that I'm traveling through something akin to an enormous wilderness.

Sixteen miles later I'm in Crook, another metropolis boasting 109 people along with a gas station, a public well on the common, and a picnic table in the shade. Water and shade are all I need. I pump water into my bottles and rest. Crook, named in honor of a post- Civil War military commander, is a prime place for lunch.

At this point I have no idea what's ahead, when I can find water, shade, or even humans. There's only one more town before I'll get to Sterling, so 16 miles later I pull into the town of Iliff, named in recognition of Colorado's first cattle king. It is furnace-like hot, the only store is long shuttered, there's no shade, and the town's water pump is padlocked. There is a post office, and while it's closed for the day, the lobby's open and provides much welcome relief from the heat and sun.

My body temperature lowered, I pedal west. It's mid-afternoon when I finally reach Sterling, where 14,000 people live, the only city within scores of miles. The skies are darkening, and I feel the impending storm. I have no idea where I'm going to sleep, have no money, but I'm remarkably calm. Waiting for the traffic light to turn, I spot two police cars in the shopping center parking lot. I bike across, greet one of the policemen and ask, "Can you tell me where the

Cabela's is? I hear they provide free camping."

"It's 40 miles north of here," he tells me. "But there's a Walmart in town." Definitely a camping possibility. I thank him and as I'm riding off think, what if I were a black man? I'm sure I never would have approached them.

It's only mid-afternoon and I decide to go to the library. I have to make a decision about money. Even camping in parks isn't free and eventually I'll have to buy food. I'm in a city 2,000 miles away from home with no cash, know no one, and don't have a credit card. I call Visa. I'm put on hold for long time periods, have my calls transferred to multiple departments, and wait for calls back as I try get cash and help paying for a place to stay. I never get cash, but they do pay for a motel room tonight. After that, good luck to me. The next day is July 4th. Visa and banks will be closed. Fretting's not going to help.

I decide to have my friends at Visa send a replacement card to a Warm Showers host in Fort Collins. With lots of Warm Showers hosts in Fort Collins and knowing that the card will not arrive on the 4th, I figure I can always stay with another host in Fort Collins while waiting for the card's arrival. Maybe I'll have my first night of stealth camping.

The motel I choose is being renovated and I appreciate the owner's going through the extra rigamarole to accommodate me. He has to deal the Visa people too. When he hears of my plan to ride to

BIKING, LESSONS, BLESSINGS AND BEER

Fort Collins the next day, he offers me five small bottles of water. Damn the weight. I'm heading into the Pawnee Grasslands and I've been warned that there may be no services until Fort Collins, 102 miles away. I'm not worried, but I have a tad more trepidation than normal. Just another day on the Great Plains. I cook dinner in the motel room; I don't have money to go out to eat even if I wanted to. I watch tv and set my alarm for 4:30 a.m. in order to get my earliest start yet.

July 3, 2017

Sterling to Fort Collins, Colorado – 103 miles

After packing, I scrounge up enough change from my handlebar pack to buy a large cup of McDonald's coffee, any size for 99¢. In the early dawn light, I chat with a dude outside McD's and quickly drink my joe. I want to get in as many miles as I can in while it's still cool. A monster day looms ahead, a century ride with no support. I prepare for the worst: heat, distance, no shade, no facilities, and a new challenge: no money.

The ride does not start easily as I climb out of Sterling into the Pawnee National Grasslands. A steady wind, tumbleweeds blowing across the road, long-abandoned oil derricks, and miles of endless grassland are my companions. What is now a sea of grass was once filled with hopeful frontier families venturing westward in their wagons. Motivated by the Homestead Act, by 1890, six million settlers reached the western plains. The harsh winters and droughts made growing crops extremely difficult. Today there is nary a sign of those adventurous souls nor anyone else for that matter.

The ride is as hard as I imagined, and it's only early morning. I hope that my water, my energy, and my bike hold up. At the 35 mile mark a sign tells me I'm in Raymer, but there's no sign of a town nor any of the 91 people who live within its confines.

Then I spot the Pawnee Station Restaurant on the other side of the road. It looks deserted, but there's a car in the parking lot. I pull in and the door's open. Yee Ha! The joint's dark and empty except for two folks hanging out at a table. It's the opportunity to fill my water bottles that makes me happy. I still have 67 miles before I get to Fort Collins and no telling where or if there'll be another place to get water. I interrupt the conversation of a man and woman working and/or living here and ask for water. The guy points to the sink. I start telling them about my lack of money, lost credit card, and stop. I wanted to let them know that I'd like to patronize their restaurant but can't. I imagine these folks think I'm looking for a handout. After all, who bikes out here with no money? But it's the truth and now I'm out of change.

BIKING, LESSONS, BLESSINGS AND BEER

The ride across the prairie continues, uneventfully, which I guess is as good as it gets as I tick off the miles at a medium pace. I stop when I reach sign announcing that down a long driveway, literally in the middle of the prairie, is Prairie School, Home of the Mustangs. I can't begin to fathom what it would be like to attend school or work here. If the wind's like this in the summer, what would outside recess be like in the winter? Brutal. I continue pedaling west and soon have my first sighting of the Rockies. Even though the mountains are still a ways off, they are a very welcome sight. The last real hills I experienced were the cloud-covered Adirondacks, and they certainly weren't snowcapped like these. After so many days of cycling through the hot, flat midwest and plains, I'm excited about the mountains, long climbs and all.

Thirty miles later, I pass through the nearly mile-high unincorporated town of Briggsdale with its post office, locked water pump, and nothing else in plain sight. Onward. I'm making progress with the hazy Rockies getting closer, and I'm ever-closer to surviving this trek through the great prairie. Twenty miles later, I smile when I reach Ault and am greeted by a "Welcome to A Unique Little Town" sign. It really is a town with plenty of stores, including my favorite, a convenience store. Having no money, I fill my bottles with mostly water and add lemonade from the machine, my first theft.

A locked well in Briggsdale

I'm in civilization. I've made it through 250-plus miles, barren stretches and have only 20 miles left to Fort Collins. I'm quite pleased with my efforts and also excited. Colorado has an allure for us Easterners, and a much more hip and outdoorsy reputation than Nebraska, Iowa, Illinois, and Indiana combined.

As I enter the outskirts of Fort Collins and near my hosts' house, I consider my status: I have no money, I'm about to be a guest at strangers' home, and I'm going to tell them that I expect mail to be delivered to their house. From all appearances this looks suspicious. But I feel like there's nothing to agonize about. Worrying won't help and frankly, what choices do I have? I'm reminded of a Yiddish story about a farmer and his horse.

One day a farmer's horse runs away. His neighbor comes over and commiserates, "I'm so sorry about your horse." And the

BIKING, LESSONS, BLESSINGS AND BEER

farmer says, "Who knows what's good or bad?" The neighbor is confused because this is clearly terrible. The horse is the most valuable thing the farmer owns. But the horse comes back the next day and he brings with him 12 feral horses. The neighbor comes back over to celebrate, "Congratulations on your great fortune!" And the farmer replies again, "Who knows what's good or bad?" The next day, the farmer's son is taming one of the wild horses when he's thrown and breaks his leg. The neighbor comes back over, "I'm so sorry about your son. This is awful." The farmer repeats, "Who knows what's good or bad?" Sure enough, the next day the army comes through their village and is conscripting able-bodied young men to go and fight in war, but the son is spared because of his broken leg.

This parable is the story my trip. I find the house of my next hosts tucked into an old neighborhood next to Colorado State University. Marney and Bob are amazing. In their 70s and retired, they lead vibrant lives. They're avid bikers and tourers. They both are great conversationalists, speak Spanish, served in the Peace Corps in Guatemala almost 50 years ago, are proud grandparents, and Bob went to Dartmouth College, 4 miles from my home. We have lots in common.

I'm immediately made to feel most welcome in their home. When I tell them about my credit card fiasco, Bob lends me $50 without my asking and tells me I can stay until the card arrives. What world am I living in? They don't even know me. Every time I have what seems to be a setback, I'm showered with kindness and generosity.

Marney and Bob

Bob and Marney invite me to accompany them to a friend's Fourth of July party soon after I arrive. No matter how long the day has been and how exhausted I am, I stay in character and say yes. We drive (the only time we get in the car during my visit) to the party, and of course I'm made to feel right at home. There's food, drink, and friendly folks galore.

On the deck out back, I'm introduced to Steve. He brought a mini-keg from work, New Belgium Brewery. Hot damn. We start talking and Steve is interested in my trip, very interested. I'm a little uneasy until Steve tells me that he rode cross-country 30 years ago starting from his home in Seattle with a woman he had just met. They

BIKING, LESSONS, BLESSINGS AND BEER

started as friends, got married, had a daughter, divorced, and now he has a wife and two young children. A little older than me, I can tell he's quite nostalgic. Steve wants me to visit the brewery, gives me his number, and I tell him I'll certainly try. I've never toured a brewery.

After the party, Marney, Bob, and I wait until dusk to bike to town for delicious, locally made ice cream and then watch fireworks from atop a parking garage. The display is a bit far away, but I'm tired and enjoy hanging with Bob and Marney more than the show. I discover Bob knew my cousin, Paul, who played football with him at Dartmouth 50 years ago. I do an online search and discover that Bob was a stud, an all-league player. Bob and Marney tell me that they come back to Dartmouth every so often for reunions. Here is when I make my second faux pas (my first being the barista and Trump). One of their Dartmouth friends, a classmate of Bob's, worked at a school where I was principal. It's a small world after all. Leo's a good guy and likable who became a teacher later in life. In his words, "I'm a good soldier. I help out at car washes, cookouts, trips..." Unfortunately, his lessons were a mess and his classroom management so poor that I didn't recommend that the school board renew his contract. Why did I tell Marney and Bob this? Stupid! But they don't seem to react, and I hope this sentence vanishes into the ether.

I'm given a bedroom on the top floor, we speak Spanish, I do laundry, and I have access to food. I feel at ease like I was in Iowa City with Jim and Lisa, and Columbus with my cousin, Lori.

July 4, 2017

Fort Collins, Colorado – 0 miles

Since I have to stay in Fort Collins to wait my credit card, I relax. There will be no miles gained today and that's absolutely fine on this gorgeous July morning. Marney leads me around the campus, and we tour the fabulous flower gardens. I decide to chillax in Old Town: read, write, watch people. As I bike out of Bob and Marney's drive I notice I have a flat tire, my first. I've traveled 2,000 miles before getting a flat, and it couldn't have happened in a better place.

After fixing the flat, I find a shady bench in Old Town. Five minutes later a neatly dressed gent with the *New York Times* under his arm asks,

"Do you mind if I share your bench?"

"Not at all," I respond and scoot over. He replies, "Thanks, you'll make me look good." I laugh and remark that I'm a scruffy looking biker. Since my bike is free of my gear, I'm not the obvious tourist. I like Milt right away and the feeling's mutual.

BIKING, LESSONS, BLESSINGS AND BEER

Milt

We talk and talk and talk some more. We chat about ourselves, I get a history and politics lesson about Russia and Crimea (he lived there for many years), his work, his sort of girlfriend, his goal to live in 100 places, philosophy, leadership, hiring ("hire people who smile and want to try new things"), travel, books, and on and on. I tell him about my lost credit card, and he offers me money, which I decline, but I'm touched.

Two hours pass and he wants his girlfriend to come by. We talk for another two hours and Irena shows up. and the three of us go to lunch at a brewpub. Milt's treat, he insists. Milt orders a tomato beer, something I've never even heard of. He lets me taste it and it's not bad. Irena and I get local drafts. While we wait for our lunches to arrive, I mistakenly drink some of her beer and am quite embarrassed. They laugh and it's all good, very good. After lunch we go to the same local ice cream shop that I went to last night. This is the life.

July 5, 2017
Fort Collins and Loveland, Colorado

Not expecting the credit card to arrive today, I take a bike ride to Loveland via the Horsetooth Reservoir. It's a fine jaunt along bike paths filled with commuters, joggers, walkers, and other bikers. The pavement to the reservoir and Loveland is smooth, as is cruising sans panniers. Loveland has a character that's grittier than Fort Collins, but I can't stay too long; Steve invited me to join him at a small lake for a picnic with his family and friends.

I get there while the party is underway, and we drink more delicious beer and I enjoy my first paddleboard ride. It's all chill until the skies get dark, my signal to go before the thunderstorm. Next, it's on to volunteer at the food shelf where Marney is a regular helper. It's an impressive facility and operation with a positive vibe. The huge warehouse looks brand new, but they've already outgrown it. Food insecurity is rampant, and even though many of the clients are well dressed, they need assistance. I unload healthy fruit snacks and break down boxes. To wrap up the afternoon, I go to New Belgium for my tour. Steve gives me a hat, "Life's a Ride, Bring Good Beer," I tour

BIKING, LESSONS, BLESSINGS AND BEER

the brewery, learn a lot about this progressive company and beer, and sample quite a few. I'm beginning to feel like part of the Fort Collins community.

After the tour Bob calls to let me know my credit card arrived. Hot damn! I zip to Bob and Marney's home, another BUI, this one without a crash. It's close to 5 p.m., I want cash before heading out tomorrow, and don't want to get a late start waiting for the banks to open in the morning. I race to a Chase Bank, figuring it will be easiest to get cash from them and make sure my card is legit.

I get to the bank just before closing time. As I wait in line, the only teller is taking forever with a customer. What's the hold up? I'm hyped after having no money for some time even though there's really no need for me to be amped up since I'm inside the bank. As I approach the counter, I hear the customer on the phone speaking Spanish to who, I assume is a bilingual representative on the other end. No wonder the delay.

I needn't have worried. My card works, I get my cash and am ready to roll.

AMOS KORNFELD

July 6, 2017

Fort Collins to Walden, Colorado – 110 miles

Today I'll ride up and over my first western pass and likely cover a century to boot. We don't have passes in the East. We've got gaps and notches and none over 5,000 feet, much less than the 10,000-footer I'll climb today. However, there's a saying us Easterners have about folks in the West: they've never met a hill that doesn't deserve a switch-back. In the East we go straight up. On a loaded bike I won't mind the switchbacks at all.

Westward, Ho!

Before I can leave, Bob wants to have coffee with me, so he gets up at 5 and makes us fresh coffee. I had already planned to meet Milt at a nearby coffee place at 6, Steve wanted to say goodbye and give me

BIKING, LESSONS, BLESSINGS AND BEER

a few bike shirts, so in keeping with being a gracious guest, I have my first coffee of the day with Bob in his kitchen. I thank him for an incredible stay and extraordinary generosity.

Milt and I meet about a mile away at a nearby coffee shop. I have money and a credit card, so for once I can treat. In a bit Steve shows up and then Bob pops in with the reflective vest I left in his house. I'm able to connect my three new Fort Collins friends. How cool is this? Still, after 3 days in Fort Collins, it is time to move on.

With mixed emotions I leave my three buds in the coffee shop. I'm reinvigorated, off I go into the great blue yonder. This time I won't be pedaling through endless prairies, but over the Rocky Mountains. It begins as a gorgeous ride up Poudre Canyon alongside the Poudre River. The sun is shining, there's no wind, and only a gradual incline. I feel great.

Thirty miles later it's quite a bit warmer, so when I see a woman watering her garden, I pull into her driveway and ask if I can have some water. I figure I'll use her hose, but she takes my two water bottles and Camelback into the house. I snap her photo as she's carrying them back. I've missed documenting too many other acts of kindness, although photos can be intrusive and awkward. Especially now. The woman covers her face and explains that she doesn't want her photo taken. Later today she's going to court. I can't recall the term she uses but essentially, she's covering her past so that her ex-husband will not be able to find her. Wow.

The first hours of Poudre Canyon; delightful cycling

I thank her for the water and wish her well. As I ride, a Colorado cyclist pulls up alongside me; it's always a treat to have two-wheeled company. Chuck's an eastern transplant and tells me how much he loves biking in Colorado. A forest fire just closed roads where he was in Breckenridge. Avoiding fire was not a concern that had entered my mind. Geese, hail, fire, what else haven't I anticipated? Eventually Chuck peels off and the road starts climbing. And then climbs some more getting significantly steeper.

The gentle 50 miles I just rode up the canyon are a memory. I slow down as the incline continues to increase, the air becomes cooler, and the sky darker. I keep on, realizing how deceived I was. I figured that since it was 60 miles from Fort Collins to Cameron Pass it would be a gradual climb, reinforced by the perfect first 50 miles. The last

BIKING, LESSONS, BLESSINGS AND BEER

10 are making me pay, in spades. You'd think I'd be used to this. A day that started so well is bound to bring adversity later.

I'm in the Arapaho and Roosevelt National Forests, the Northern Front Range of the Rocky Mountains, surrounded by trees too small and scruffy to provide shelter and protection at nearly 9,000 feet when I feel a light drizzle. Great. I spot a driveway blocked by a gate with a cabin out back, worth checking out. It doesn't look like anyone's here, so I open the gate and roll the bike to the back of the cabin. Sheets of rain fall while I hang out under the eaves staying mostly dry.

Waiting out the rain climbing towards Cameron Pass

Fifteen minutes pass and the rain lets up. The likelihood that I will see sun and not be in the clouds at this elevation is slim to none. This ought to be fun. I crawl a few more miles and pull into a national forest campground. It's primitive; just car camping spots and not much else. I don't want to set up my tent this early in the day as I'd end up laying in my sleeping bag trying to stay warm. The only shelter I see is the bathroom. Déjà vu. I have a snack and decide to continue making my way up to Cameron Pass. As soon as I start climbing, the rain falls again. The grade is getting even steeper, the air colder, so I turn around and go back to the campground to wait out the rain under the bathroom entrance. When it ceases, I resume my climb.

I'm pedaling the hardest I have thus far on this trip. Not only is it extremely steep, I'm at high altitude. There are few cars, so when the road is straight enough that I can see ahead and behind, I started tacking back and forth using both lanes. My legs and lungs burn. One more turn, I tell myself, and I'll be at the top. Nope. The next turn I'll be at the pass. Nope. No matter how much I hope, I just keep climbing and burning. I pass Joe Wright Reservoir. More turns, more climbing. I see snow covered peaks in the distance. Then I see a green sign. Eventually I'm close enough that I can read it. Cameron Pass, 10,276 feet.

I made it. I'm pumped but I'm not going to savor the victory here. I haven't the energy, it's damn cold and I don't want to get chilled. As I bike down a wicked long, steep descent it starts raining again and I pull under a logging shed.

BIKING, LESSONS, BLESSINGS AND BEER

At 10,267 feet, Cameron Pass kicked my ass

When the rain lightens to a drizzle, I resume riding and then turn into a state campground, I talk to the woman at the entrance booth and let her know that I'm considering camping here. It's still cold, I'm still at high elevation, and it still feels too early to hunker down. My mood has become as gray as the weather. I bid the attendant adieu, follow the Sirens' song, and choose to ride on.

I fly into and out of Gould, a town in bygone days, and now just a nam on the map and continue north. The sun comes out, and for the first time since the Adirondacks, the sun is a good friend, warming me from the cold, damp air. The road flattens and now I'm feeling great, optimistic. I know that Walden's a town where I can camp in the park, and staying at 8,000 feet ought to be a lot warmer than 10,000 feet. For once, listening to the Sirens proves to be the right call.

I'm psyched when I see the sign welcoming me to Walden, Colorado, population 602. Although extremely remote, it's the only true town within God-knows-where and has two gas stations, a grocery store, dollar store, school, and even an airport. Just past the welcome to Walden sign, I miss the sharp left and end up in the parking lot of an old school overlooking an enormous basin, a sliver of 16,000-square-mile North Park.

I head back to where I missed the turn when I spot an older couple seated on their porch. I stop and ask the pair if they know how to get to the camping area. Walden's on the TransAmerica bike trail, so I'm sure this community is familiar with bike tourers. The gentleman motions for me to come up and join them on the porch. He offers me lemonade as I sit and am introduced to John and his wife, Roberta. John is revving to go. He begins by telling me about the town, places to sleep, and the high school reunion they just hosted. Almost everyone from their graduation class is still around 50 years later. Roberta tells me they've occasionally had a biker camp on their lawn. Seems like a hint that I'm welcome to stay here.

Even though their lawn is astroturf, they seem like good folk, it's getting late, and it's not like I have better options. I'll get more local flavor than sleeping in a park. Besides, I am beat, really beat. Cameron Pass kicked my ass. Not knowing exactly what transpired, I'm not

BIKING, LESSONS, BLESSINGS AND BEER

invited to sleep on the astroturf but in their house. *Don't ask and you shall receive.*

Roberta and John in Walden, North Park

My quarters are one of the several rooms in their finished downstairs that house their kids and grandkids when they visit. I unpack, get a shower in my own bathroom, and John takes me out to the shed to store the bike. Now he wants to give me a tour of Walden and North Park. What can I say?

Off we go in his pick-up truck, and although I'm certainly interested, I'm exhausted. First, John gives me a tour of the downtown area. We stop at his old house and he introduces me to one of his sons who now lives here with his family. John Junior writes for the local newspaper and cuts hair. We drive out of town and John shows me where his dad once worked, old mining sites, former railroads, fishing holes, the lake, telling me stories the whole time.

We visit one of his oldest friends. As the sun is setting, the moon is rising. It is stunning.

All the while, John tells stories, G-rated ones. He could write a book about the million-acre North Park knowing like he does. He's lived here his whole life except for several years when he attended Colorado State. He's so into sharing his world that even though I've been fighting to stay awake, I love listening to his stories. What kind of guest would I be if I fell asleep? Finally, as darkness sets in at 9, we head back to John and Roberta's house. Roberta made spaghetti, garlic bread, and veggies for dinner. They say a prayer that includes wishing me safe travels, I give an amen and enjoy a delicious, home-cooked meal. And the day's circle is complete: breakfast with friends, a sweet ride turned harsh then smooth, and a splendid evening with new friends.

Wyoming

July 7, 2017

Walden, Colorado to Rawlins, Wyoming – 112 miles

Again I'm taken by the tremendous expanses of the West. Fort Collins was an anomaly. There is literally nothing between Walden and the next town, Riverside, other than enormous ranches. I know the word awesome is overused, but taken literally it means "extremely impressive or daunting; inspiring great admiration, apprehension, or fear." I am full of awe. Since Ogallala, I have been cruising through the biggest landscape I've ever been in. I can see for hundreds of miles in all directions. It's as if Vermont could be neatly tucked into these vistas.

I make my first and only turn, 10 miles out of Walden and see a biker ahead. It's the first one I've seen since yesterday morning and kind of odd as there's no one else out here, including cars. As I get closer, I see that the biker is pulling a Burley trailer. I catch him and we stop and talk while we both shed layers.

At 8,000 feet it's quite chilly at dawn but warms up quickly as the sun rises. I tell him he's the first tourer I've seen in ages; he tells me there are several others who camped with him last night in the city park. Burley Boy tells me about one strange biker dude who got up at 3 a.m. in order to get an early start. The guy's in some sort of race. There's no way Burley Boy's going to keep up with me, so I bid him a good ride and head deeper into Wyoming.

Before leaving home, I created a bunch of playlists on my phone, but I've seldom used them. Most of the time I don't want to listen; I'd rather be taking in the surroundings, visually and auditorily. However, I knew from a few rides at home and my John Muir Trail hike that there are times when music can provide a burst of energy or serve as a welcome distraction. The conditions have to be right: few cars, good visibility, and a shoulder. This morning is one of those times. I pedal amid ranch land on all sides and jam to rock 'n' roll from my younger days. It's a long haul between amenities.

Fifty miles after starting this morning, I reach Riverside. I'm

BIKING, LESSONS, BLESSINGS AND BEER

sitting on a bench outside a restaurant when a touring cyclist pulls in. His name is Doug and he tells me he got up in Walden at 3 this morning to start biking but was so cold that he spent the rest of the night in the post office lobby. Doug is the cyclist Burley Boy told me about. Doug's doing the TransAm race, but due to a work issue, he had to fly home for a bit. He's also going east to west although the actual race is west to east. Huh?

I watched a documentary about the TransAm bike race. It's much cooler, though not as well-known, as the older RAAM (Race Across America). On the TransAm, bikers travel like I am, self-supported. The TransAm starts in Washington state, ends in Virginia, and follows Adventure Cycling's TransAmerica route, the same path I have just joined. Race winners have completed the 4,200 miles in 17 days.

Doug goes to the restaurant for a meal; I finish my drink and snack and pedal on. I have a Warm Showers stay in Saratoga, "glamping" is how the host describes it. She has a camper where I could sleep like I did in Blue Mountain. I arrive in Saratoga early in the afternoon, too early to end the day as the cycling conditions today have been superb. I'm feeling good, resting often enough, and there isn't wind. Saratoga is home to the public Hobo Hot Springs and folks whom I chat with at the store tell me it's worth the visit. Even though the idea of hot springs on a scorching summer day seems odd, I have time and figure, why not?

Hobo Hot Springs

Hobo Hot Springs is just a hop, skip, and a jump from the middle of town and is unlike any hot springs I've been in. The pool is owned and maintained by the Town of Saratoga. It's open 24 hours a day all year long, the bath house has showers and restroom facilities, and it's FREE to the public. Even if the springs are too hot for a soak on this toasty summer day, warm, pooled spots in the river are soothing.

A local guy gives me a bunch of watermelon chunks, delish. Definitely worth the stop. Before leaving the springs, I check my map. It is 20 miles until... my first interstate bike ride. Being a bike rider from the east, I've long fantasized about biking on an interstate. When it's closed to cars. The notion of biking alongside cars and trucks at interstate speeds in Wyoming? Unimaginable, yet that's what I'm about to do.

There is no other way to go; this is the Adventure Cycling route.

BIKING, LESSONS, BLESSINGS AND BEER

Thinking about the 11 miles from Walcott to Sinclair on I-80 is giving me the heebie jeebies. Before the death ride, I stop at the gas station located at the bottom of the highway ramps. It is different in so many ways than than the convenience stores in small towns. This one is isolated, off a dirt drive, and the interstate is its only neighbor. There are no locals here nor is there any midwestern warmth.

I buy a cold drink, eat a candy bar, and send out a farewell Facebook post about my impending descent into madness. It's time to ride Interstate 80. I've paralleled this cross-country highway through numerous states and crossed over it many a time. It's responsible for reducing traffic on roads I've biked, especially the Lincoln Highway. Now I'm about to take on the beast, even if it is for only 11 miles. The wind's at my back so biking at 15 miles per hour should get me to my exit in 45 minutes or so.

As soon as I bike up the entrance ramp, I'm smack dab in a construction zone. Unlike state roads where construction projects are my friends, I'm in a maze. Signs and concrete barriers are everywhere. I bike through the gauntlet. Cars and truck are a blur. I can't pay attention to the traffic pattern. The shoulder's now the lane. I ride as far to the right as I can and fear what I've gotten myself into.

Maybe the construction is a blessing, a way for me to ease into interstate riding as cars and trucks are going slower than normal due to the barriers. The construction ends in a few minutes and I have my shoulder back. The posted speed limit is 75 miles per hour.

I relax a bit and am surprised to find myself not overly anxious, although very much on guard. The wide shoulder and rumble strip help. As I ride, vehicles tend to move over to the left lane. Whether it's because I'm in Wyoming, it's Saturday afternoon, or both, there's a steady flow, but the cars and trucks are spaced apart. I must admit, this is much better than I anticipated. In some ways this is actually cool. I'm riding my bike on a freaking interstate highway, legally too, while it's open to cars and trucks.

I-80 continues all the way to Sacramento, though probably not legal to bike, and the amount of cars and noise would not be fun for long. However, it feels much safer than a number of other roads I've ridden. As I ponder this, I notice a car pulled over in the shoulder ahead, in my lane! Are they kidding? I pass them and then come to an historic site, a rest area, and before too long, I'm at the Sinclair exit. That wasn't so bad. *Like most things in life, the unknown is often scarier than reality.* Stopping at the Sinclair gas station and truck stop, I think that I shouldn't have posted before I got on the freeway. I better let the world know I made it safely. I also want to decompress, cool off, and check the map.

I plop myself on a stool in front of the window, open a package of chocolate pop tarts, and take out my phone and map. There's only me and one other person in the truck stop dining room. Ahhhhhh.

BIKING, LESSONS, BLESSINGS AND BEER

My heart rate and respiration are normal. I survived, nay, flourished during my ride on I-80. When the truckstop restaurant has done what it can for me, I head to the store section of the complex to fill my water bottles and Camelback with Powerade. I stand at the counter, motion to my liquid containers, and tell the clerk,

"I filled these with Powerade. How much?"

The clerk answers, "Water, right?"

I say, "No, Powerade and…" He interrupts me and smiles.

"Water? No charge."

I have 7 miles left to Rawlins, home to 9,000 folks, a few RV campgrounds, and a Walmart. I've been told that Walmart is the biggest employer in 20 of our states, and as I ride through rural America, I hear folks talking about the stores as if they are status symbols. To some, it means that their neck of the woods is important enough, at least populated enough, to have a Walmart. We have a Walmart 10 miles away and I never thought about it this way.

Tonight may be my first time camping in a Walmart campground, something I've considered but the opportunity hasn't yet presented itself. I'm not sure why I'm so intrigued by this. Walmart provides free camping, typically for RVs, and it just seems like something I ought to try. When I get to Rawlins, my Walmart dreams are dashed; this Walmart is smack dab between the main drag and the interstate, and I can't imagine getting much sleep in these environs. I bike into town where a small streetfest is winding down, listen to a rock 'n' roll band, and then ride up the hill to the KOA campground. I pay my money to the clerk in exchange for the code to enter the bathroom and sleep on a patch of grass at the back of an enormous RV-filled lot, take a bag of popcorn, and head to the designated "tenting area."

After I shower and set up, Burley Boy, aka Marty whom I met this morning outside Walden, pulls in. I'm surprised to see him since I know I'm riding much faster than him until I realize I've been in Rawlins for four hours. Marty's a friendly New York transplant who's mostly retired, a bit younger than me, and does lots of touring. He is clearly "biking his own bike." His pace is slow because he's in no hurry, he just tours. He and I are the only ones at the tent area, and I enjoy the company of a fellow biker as we tell stories while we cook and eat our separate dinners. I doubt I'll see him again, but I thought the same thing this morning. I watch the moon rise and the sun set. There are worse places to camp.

BIKING, LESSONS, BLESSINGS AND BEER

July 8, 2017

Rawlins to Lander, Wyoming – 125 miles

I've got 45 miles to go before any services or guaranteed shade, so riding early in the day is key once again. It's 125 miles to Lander, the next significant population center and today's target. After passing a sizable strip of old motels, I come to the Wyoming Frontier Prison Museum, the elementary school, and Gun Club Road with signs pointing to the Rawlins Outdoor Shooting Complex. That could be a neat stop but I'm sure it's not open at this early hour, so I ride on. That's it. There's nothing in front of me, to my left, to my right, or behind me except for Wyoming prairie, high plains, and fence. Half of Wyoming is federal lands, so I know I can stop and camp most anywhere. I continue to resist that notion, set a daily target and almost always hit it. I usually enjoy being around people after a day alone in the saddle, especially at night.

The road's awful, the shoulder is bumpy and cracked, so I only ride it when I hear a car behind me. Otherwise I ride in the lane. Thankfully the road is nearly free of vehicles. I'm pretty much alone early this morning. The landscape is dull and when I come to the 3 Forks-Muddy Gap Service Station several hours later, I've covered 45 miles. This is the first and only place to refill my water and get something to eat now and for the foreseeable future. The service station and convenience store is Muddy Gap; there's nothing else here. Somewhere around here are 104 people living within a 30-mile radius, but where? I can't see any sign of human habitation other than the woman working the register who tells me that she lives above the store. The station's situated at a T in the road: right goes to Casper, left eventually will take me to the Tetons and Yellowstone. I enjoy a microwaveable cup of mac and cheese. Amazing what one will eat and enjoy on a trip like this. I psych myself up for the next stretch of vast, Wyoming open space.

I'm more concerned with water than shade or camping. I share the High Plains with sky, rocks, and sporadic cars. There must be animals and other living creatures, but I don't see or hear them. After a few hours of riding up and down hills and past scenic rock formations, I'm in Jeffrey City. I thought the towns in the midwest were depressed, but Jeffrey City is a ghost town, figuratively and almost literally. Once a thriving uranium mining town that was home to over 1,000 residents, now there are only 58 people living here. Someone wrote, "Jeffrey City sits forgotten, forlorn, rotting away in the Wyoming sun, rain and snow." It may be worse than a ghost town; people still live here.

Some of the dilapidated buildings, like the gas station, motel, and a store, are mostly standing, their signs lay on the ground. It feels

BIKING, LESSONS, BLESSINGS AND BEER

depressing, even in the bright sunshine. I stop in the one gas station and restaurant still standing, buy a soda and chips, and sit on the shaded porch eating my lunch of tuna, chips, and carrots. The more I eat out of my panniers, the less weight I carry.

My next stop will be Sweetwater Station, 43 miles away and I have no idea what I'll find. I do know it'll be hot in the afternoon, as always. Sure enough, I arrive in Sweetwater in the middle of the afternoon, it's extremely hot, and the humidity as well as the wind are picking up. Sweetwater Station is all of a rest area, a well-appointed one at that, with clean, cold water and shade. That's all there is, that and the Mormon Handcart Site and Visitor Center just down the road. Nothing else until Lander. Ho boy.

After the break I ride, and soon reach the height of the land and spot snow on distant peaks. There's wind pushing me back and it's bumming me out a bit. It's not Indiana or Nebraska headwind, but it's rough late in the day. I begin to descend when my wheels stick to the road and I almost tumble. What the? The highway shoulder's patched with a tarry substance, soft and gooey from the heat. This is going to be a heckuva downhill. Luckily there aren't many cars, so I ride in the lane to avoid the sticky tar. It's a nasty downhill, a few miles long and I use the brakes frequently and ride slowly.

A mega-long day plus heat, wind, and now a crappy riding surface. What else can make this harder? I round a sharp bend and find out. Lightning flashes in the not-too-distant sky. Freakin' A! I pedal faster, tar be damned. I see more lightning bolts ahead and feel a few drops of rain. I'm heading into darkening skies right towards the tempest. Because this scenario isn't daunting enough, there's absolutely no shelter in sight, no buildings, no trees, no side roads, nothing. Wyoming. I pedal as fast as I can, driven by fear.

I'm living my worst nightmare, cycling in a thunderstorm without refuge. I'm either going to find a ditch or culvert to crawl into or beat the storm. There's a third possibility. I could get hit by lightning. Most people survive but I'd rather not find out. It feels like the John Muir Trail all over again.

A few summers ago, I was in California backpacking the John Muir Trail, reputed to be the most scenic 225-mile section of the Pacific Crest Trail. Hiking the JMT means walking through one magnificent valley after another, climbing consecutive passes that grow in elevation from 9,000 feet in Yosemite and finishing at over 14,000 feet atop Mt. Whitney. The Sierra Nevada Mountains are known to be rain-free in the summer, getting all their precipitation in the form of 300 inches of annual snowfall. That's been my experience having been there a number of times. If there ever is summer rain, it comes in the form of a rare afternoon thunderstorm. Except that summer.

Old timers told us that they hadn't seen a weather system like

BIKING, LESSONS, BLESSINGS AND BEER

the one we were experiencing in 50 years. It lasted for most of 3 consecutive days. At noon on the third day of the rain, I climbed up 13,000-foot Forrester Pass. It was cloudy but not raining and there was no thunder. We knew it was risky since we had thunderstorms the past 2 days, but unsure if the next day would be clear, we hiked on. We summitted the pass and looked south to where we were headed, not too dark. For the next 4 miles the trail switch-backed then straightened out until it reached tree line. If a storm came, we were screwed.

As we rounded the bend, we looked east. Uh oh. The skies were black, and with loaded backpacks we booked it as fast as we could down the switchbacks, not nearly as quickly as I would have liked. Two miles later we were done with the steep section and were in wide open, stone-littered fields. Thunder claps boomed above, and we watched the dark clouds rapidly approach. Terrified, we caught up to two other frightened hikers and encouraged them to book it. We ran-hiked as fast as we could which wasn't a run but much faster than a walk.

Then lightning bolts zapped ahead of us, close to the ground. Shit! This was not heat lightning. More bolts. It looked like what you'd see in a cartoon, but this was real. We felt the electricity. We smelled it. I've never been that close to being hit. We couldn't go back. The only thing to do was motor to the trees, probably another half-mile away. More lightning and cracks of thunder nearby. We sprinted and made it to a stand of trees where we joined a few guys with horses and packs. Moments later, the couple we had passed arrived, out of breath and shaking. They panted, "We were almost hit. Right in front of us..." We all waited in the cold rain under a stand of trees until the thunderstorm paused.

Now, a few years later, I'm biking as fast as I can towards Lander. There are still flashes of lightning illuminating the sky ahead, but they haven't come any closer. I keep pumping, feeling no effects of having ridden 115 miles thus far today. I see a T junction ahead and then make out a sign, "Twin Pines RV Park and Campgrounds" just off to the right. Shelter! I relax and coast over to the park, stash the bike under the building's eaves and head into the office, overcome with relief.

It's still afternoon and I don't want to sleep here. I want to get to the Lander city park, but I am enjoying this sanctuary. The woman working doesn't mind if I stick around so I buy a drink and wait in the office and then on the porch of the small, upscale RV park. I scan the northern skies in the direction of Lander and watch the deep, dark clouds.

After an hour of sitting outside the campground office, it's time to get off the pot and try for Lander. I'm out of the wilderness and can easily find refuge if the rains and lightning return. The last 9 miles

BIKING, LESSONS, BLESSINGS AND BEER

are spent riding exurban shoulders lined with houses and businesses. I've never enjoyed ugly riding more.

I roll into Lander in the early evening and follow the map's directions to the city park for free camping. There are some folks around picnicking and a few tents set are up. Lander's known for its rock climbing, mountain biking, and hiking. I set up camp and head to town where I treat myself to a Mexican dinner. I eat alone, am not successful engaging the waiter but enjoy cold beer, chips, and salsa with my burrito. Then I buy groceries and return to my campsite just before dark. There are a quite a few more tents set up nearby, but I have no conversations, not even acknowledgments. It's ironic. Here I am camping with outdoors people who could be members of my tribe, yet I don't get even a nod. Instead, it's the RV community who welcomes me into their world more than once. Go figure.

July 9, 2017

Lander to Dubois, Wyoming – 82 miles

I wake up, pack, and bike to McDonalds for my favorite: their 99-cent coffee and free Wi-Fi. Today I'll ride through the Wind River Reservation for 75 miles until I reach the next town, Dubois. As I ride out of Mickey D's parking lot, I notice I have a flat tire, my second. I'm carrying only a small bike pump for roadside flats, so I cross the street to where the city's bike shop is conveniently located. It's just after seven and the store doesn't open until 9. I hang out front in front for over an hour until a shop worker starts putting bikes outside and sees me. Even though it's not time for him to open, bike dudes have been helpful on my sojourn and he lets me in. We chat, I buy more patches and a tube, pump up my tires using their floor pump and head out for another day across the Great Plains.

Leaving Lander after the late start, I'm already climbing in the heat. Same as always. An hour and a half later I stop at a supermarket in Fort Washakie on the Wind River Indian Reservation. It looks and feels just like any other supermarket except most of the folks here are Native American, not something I've ever experienced. Nothing uncomfortable or extraordinary, just something I've never seen back East. Leaving the store, I'm back in wide-open country and the only refuge between here and Dubois is a rest area where I plan to stop for water.

I ride the 20 miles to the Diversion Dam Junction rest area without any unusual occurrences and am thoroughly enjoying Wyoming's amenities of cold water, shade, and clean restroom when who should pedal in but cross-country racer Doug. How did I get ahead of him? We wait out a brief rain shower and decide to ride together. What the hay.

BIKING, LESSONS, BLESSINGS AND BEER

I like to bike alone. I ride as far as I want and stop when I want. When I crave human connection, I find it by greeting strangers, sitting in a convenience store, and engaging with folks at a campground. If I have doubts or questions about a route or place, I can ask. On the other hand, if I were with another cyclist, I'd have someone to converse with, wonder, plan, and problem solve. It would mean I'd be less likely to interact with strangers, but sometimes I'd like the company, especially in big spaces, facing crappy weather, and when I'm tired, which often means operating with faulty judgment.

Now I'm with Doug who prefers talking to listening, or perhaps I've become a better listener than talker. Either way, I don't mind letting him do the talking. This is the same guy I met briefly a few days ago in Riverside, the one who got up at 3 in the morning and ended up sleeping in the post office lobby. The guy who is racing the TransAm, backwards.

Doug, still speaking with his native Long Island accent, lives in New Jersey and is married, and has a son who just finished college. He tells me that he's on a personal quest to better his TransAm time from the year before. Doug's one of five riders who's racing east to west, and since he's the only one of the five west-bounders still riding, he tells me he's in first place. He works for a cable company that had gone on strike, but he had to fly home recently for some meetings and now is back on the course. Ride your own ride, Doug.

While I'm pedaling a basic Specialized Diverge, Doug has the next model up, lighter and with better components. He's also traveling lightly and super aerodynamically. A bag stores gear under his handlebars, another is under his top tube and a third bag is tucked behind his seat post. He has no panniers, carries no tent, no cooking gear, and few clothes. He has a sleeping bag and bivy sack but is mostly using his credit card for accommodations and dining at restaurants. Doug is my height but outweighs me by some 60 pounds.

Not long after we leave the rest area, we come to a van stopped in our shoulder. Two young guys are outside waiting for us. They're the support crew returning from a cross country bike trip that raised money for a charity funding clean water projects in developing countries. They have lots of leftover, donated goodies, and want to give us some. For real? I'm like a kid in a candy store. They load me up with as many gels and bars as I can stuff into my packs, dozens. Doug takes only a banana, peels it and eats it. No extra weight for him.

With my packs overflowing, Doug and I ride along the Wind River. It's soon apparent why the river and mountain range are so named. Like the Erie Canal, we're in a wind tunnel but this one winds uphill. We move slowly and stop only once so Doug can put air in his tire with a cartridge and use a hose to fill his water bottles from a closed antique store. It's been an exacting day—sometimes shorter

BIKING, LESSONS, BLESSINGS AND BEER

days are the toughest. I'm happy when we finally pull into Dubois (pronounced "dew boys"), a quaint tourist town miles from anywhere, and there's a Warm Showers.

Doug and gift-bearing gents

This is a Warm Showers unlike any other I've encountered. The host is a church. I call the phone number I have, and the person who answers my call is the caretaker. He comes over, apologizes for not feeling well, gives us a quick tour of the building where we'll stay adjacent to the church, and explains the rules. It's a sweet set-up: we have a kitchen, several rooms, and a bathroom—our own guesthouse. He informs us that there's a meeting here the next morning so we shouldn't be alarmed when a cook arrives at 5 a.m. Then he's off. I set up in the living room while Doug takes the other room.

While I cook dinner on the kitchen stove, Doug tells me he's going to a restaurant across the street for dinner and asks me to join him for a beer when I'm done. He dines on a buffalo burger, and I drink a Moose Drool beer described by the brewery as "...the best American brown ale in the world. Light on the palate. Rich mahogany color..." I can't concur that it is the best but drinking anything in the Wind River range in the cool evening air after today's haul is a treat.

July 10, 2017

Dubois to Yellowstone, Wyoming – 110 miles

As forewarned, the cook arrives at 5, but it doesn't bother me as I'm mostly awake. I say good morning from under my sleeping bag and head over to introduce myself. While we chat over coffee, Kelly tells me she's a recent transplant from Michigan and loves living here, the community, even the winter. She opened a bakery in town, and I crack up when I see what she's serving the Chamber of Commerce breakfast this morning.

Doug and I head out at 5:30 a.m. with the moon setting, the sun yet to rise, and frost on the ground. It's beautiful, peaceful, and chilly even in July at 7,000 feet. Doug rode this route the year before and likes to give me advance notice of what's coming up. After telling him repeatedly that I like to be surprised, he stops. However, one thing he had repeatedly warned me about was Togwotee Pass. It's been

BIKING, LESSONS, BLESSINGS AND BEER

looming in the back of my mind since he brought it up yesterday. This gap, just shy of 10,000 feet, causes me a bit of trepidation, and I have 30 miles to think about the ascent.

Breakfast at the church in Dubois

I mentioned that Doug has an aerodynamic rig, so much so that when we descend steep hills, even into the wind, he tucks and coasts. I have to pedal, still can't keep up, and he's soon out of sight. Part of me wishes I had such a sleek set-up, but I'm not racing. The road up Togwotee is long, steep, and full of curves but not nearly as steep as Cameron Pass, nor does it burn my lungs or make me need to break. I'm in great shape and I cruise up the pass leaving Doug in the dust. I admit, like being in the lead during a race, I'm pumped. After a few turns, I look back. No Doug. Even though I haven't raced in several years, the competitive juices still flow. I look back several times on the climb but can't see Doug. Kicking Doug's butt with his fancier bike and lighter load feels great and I wait at a summit pond for him to finish.

The snow-capped Tetons. What a sight to see, especially while traveling on a bike with nothing to impede my view and moving slowly enough to take in all this beauty. We descend 3,000 feet into the valley with headwinds so powerful that I have to pedal downhill and still hover around 10 miles per hour. Meanwhile, Doug is long gone. I don't mind. These are some of the most stunning vistas I've seen and I'm in no rush.

First view of the Tetons

Doug and I plan to meet at the store in Morin, and when I see his bike set out front to catch my eye, I pull in. Doug's at a table out back and while he orders a meal, true to form, I eat my peanut butter sandwich. I sit with Doug and while he waits for his food, I recognize this as an opportune time to say so long. It's been different to have shared some of the ride, but I want it to end. Doug's a fine guy, educated, flies a glider, and is on his second cross-country jaunt. It's

BIKING, LESSONS, BLESSINGS AND BEER

just that he and I are on different paths. While I have a goal and miles to cover, I'm trying to enjoy the roses, if not always smell them. I savor meeting strangers and am often in awe of my surroundings. This isn't Doug's trip. He reminds me of his website and how to track his progress. Sure, I say, knowing well that I never will. He doesn't ask for my contact info or, come to think of it, anything about me even though it seemed like he enjoyed my company. C'est la vie.

Not long after Doug and I part, I'm at the entrance gate to Grand Teton National Park. "Yes, bikers have to pay too," the gate attendant tells me with a smile, and my fee also covers Yellowstone. The Tetons are one of my daughter's favorite places and it's easy to see why: jutting, snow-capped peaks; lakes; woods, it's all extraordinary. The park is named for Grand Teton, the tallest mountain in the range, just shy of 14,000 feet. Nineteenth-century French trappers called the mountains les trois tétons—the three teats. I'm in mythical country and it's all new to me. The only minor downside is sharing the road with many motorized vehicles.

I ride along the eastern side of Jackson Lake for miles while the majestic snow-capped Tetons reflect off the water. It's impossible to overuse adjectives. I pull off at any interesting place I choose and admire the views. It's glorious biking. Ahead I see cars slowing down and two lit road signs catch my eye.

Okay, so I have to be alert for potential drama and not just the grandeur. Later, I see t-shirts with a picture of a biker, a bear, and the words "Meals on Wheels." Ha! But I'm not laughing now.

I'm hungry again and pull into the next picnic area. As I roll in, I see a large family at the table to the left, some smoking. Off to my right is another table where a couple older than me are not puffing on cigarettes and have more room at the table. I walk my bike to the right where the pair eating lunch. I greet them, chuckle and say, "Don't worry, I have plenty of food." They welcome me while clearing space. I sit at the other end of the table, take out my food, and we begin to talk.

Before I can open my bag of bread to make a sandwich, the woman offers what remains of their lunch. There's plenty: cheese, crackers, cookies, juice. It's not only that different food is a treat, it tastes so good because it's offered by these sweet souls. They tell me about their adult kids who sound really neat, although the husband keeps referring to their eldest as a bum. She does most of the talking and it's clear that he's experiencing some form of dementia. While that strike me as sad, I'm touched by how she cares for him while calling him on his b.s. They're from southern Missouri. Staying a few hours away, they enjoy summering in Montana and drove to the park for the day. He was a country doctor back home and they must be approaching 40 years together. It's a wonderful lunchtime and I'm in a great space as I head towards Yellowstone.

BIKING, LESSONS, BLESSINGS AND BEER

A sweet, roadside lunch

I figure on riding as long as I want and then finding a place to camp, which shouldn't be too hard in a National Park. I'm not equipped for hiking or backcountry camping so staying in a campground it will be. I keep riding as the afternoon turns to evening. It's good to be in the woods replete with lakes, streams, but no campgrounds. Another example of poor planning, aka riding by the seat of my bicycle shorts.

Eventually I reach Grant Village. Village is an understatement, more like Grant City. I pass the visitor center and follow the signs to the campground. Four hundred sites, eight group sites, and a long line to check in. I lean my bike against the building and see the sign, "Campground Full." Uh oh. Burley Boy, aka Marty, told me that national parks always find a space for a biker. We'll find out. I wait in line, not too worried. Worst case, I'll stealth camp in the National Park. When it's my turn, I find out Marty's right; there is a place for me. The concessionaire at the window asks if I want to camp remotely or share a space. I'll camp with others.

I find two tents standing at the site but no one's here. After I put up my tent, my site mates arrive. One is from Vermont, the first Vermonter I've met on this expedition. And she's a school principal to boot. What are the odds? With only 300 public schools in Vermont, it's pretty slim chances and it wouldn't be unreasonable to think we may have met in the past. We haven't, and it's unlikely that I'll see her again; she's moving to Massachusetts to be closer to family.

Montana

July 11, 2017

Yellowstone, Wyoming to Earthquake Lake, Montana –

109 miles

I didn't think the ride through the Grand Tetons could be topped, but this morning Yellowstone may be doing just that. The cool, traffic-free early morning ride takes me past rivers and gorges and then the sign towards Old Faithful. I might as well see what all the fuss is about. As I pedal past Geyser Basin, an enormous bear scrambles across the road ahead of me. A grizzly? It's bigger than any black bear I've ever seen, and browner. I jump off my bike, knowing this isn't wise, but I want a closer look. When else am I going to see a grizzly bear? I need a closer look. I'm not planning to feed it or get too close, but I want a good view. I'm in Yellowstone but it doesn't feel like I'm in the wilderness. There are cars on the road and if things go south, I can jump in a vehicle. Probably. I run up the road to where I saw him scamper into the brush. I see shrubs rustle and start to follow. It's dense thicket so I stop. What am I thinking? Chasing a grizzly? I scan ahead for movement, but he's gone. I'm not going any further. I'm gonna to avoid being a meal on wheels, at least this morning.

As I approach Old Faithful from the access road, I see giant plumes of water spouting in the air. I ride closer and witness a massive eruption. Holy cow. I ride to the boardwalk and walk my bike to get as close as I can while the geyser's erupting. A ranger stops me and points to the "No Bikes" sign. Bummer. I walk my bike back and lock it up. By the time I return, the plumes are winding down. I listen to a ranger explain that Old Faithful eruptions can shoot up to 8,400 gallons of boiling water up to 185 feet high and last from a minute and a half to five minutes. Intervals between eruptions range from half-hour to two hours. He says that the next one should be better so I decide to stick around.

I walk around the smaller geysers and grand hotel and then get a seat as close as I can to the geyser. It's a beautiful sunny day and I pass

BIKING, LESSONS, BLESSINGS AND BEER

the rest of the time on the benches talking to a man who's here with his family from L.A. When Old Faithful erupts 90 minutes later, I'm somewhat disappointed that it's not as high as the prior eruption or as I anticipated. Still, it is an impressive phenomenon and great to just sit in the warm-but-not-yet-hot sun.

Old Faithful

Yellowstone is an immense park, and although I've only seen a fraction, what a phenomenal bonus it's been that it's on my route. Now it's time for Montana. Biking towards the park's western exit, I see several illuminated "Bison on the Road" signs. I am psyched to see the legendary buffalo. Bison are big, burly creatures, and because they weigh up to a ton and stand six feet tall, it's not as if they can hide. I also know they can do damage, but I've never heard of a biker being done in by a bison. I cycle and keep looking, figuring I'll stay as far away as I can when I see one. Sadly, I don't see a single bison. I do stop twice to observe herds of elk feeding by the Yellowstone River. They're large too, females weigh up to 500 pounds, males over 700, and I observe a baby suckling its mother. Watching wildlife while I bike, another benefit of this route.

I continue cycling along the river. Then, trotting across the road in front of me and a stopped car coming the other direction is a... wolf? I think it's a wolf. It crosses the road not more than 100 feet in from me and it's large; much bigger than any coyote I've ever seen. It trots into the brush and I lose sight. Like the grizzly, I'll never be able to confirm it, but it doesn't matter.

Eventually I exit the park and enter wild, rugged, Big Sky country, Montana, a state that has held an allure for many years. Added to this, my son is only 300 miles away, likely no more than three days pedaling. I'm in a great mood and why not? I just experienced Yellowstone and the Grand Tetons by bike, was not eaten by a grizzly, and physically feel great.

Near the park entrance is the tourist town of West Yellowstone. On my right is "Freeheel and Wheel" a bike shop with a coffee bar. I'm warmly greeted by the owner, we start chatting, and she makes me a coffee. Melissa is an avid biker, obviously. She tells me about her recent bike trip to Majorca, Spain describing it as a bike touring mecca.

BIKING, LESSONS, BLESSINGS AND BEER

She also confirms that in spring you can bike the roads of Yellowstone before cars are allowed and, she smiles, "it's as amazing as it sounds."

Melissa's married to a Vermonter and visits our state regularly. It's good to have like-minded company, and I'm tempted to hang a while. But it's early afternoon and I have 6 daylight hours if needed. The Sirens are singing, and West Yellowstone is a tourist town, not a place I want to hang out. Plus, Jake beckons, so after I finish my coffee and take advantage of the grocery store in town to restock, I travel on.

Melissa with a map of Majorca

With no fixed destination other than northwest towards Missoula, I keep going along a boring stretch of state highway. It's hot as I pass turn offs to campgrounds and keep on. In 10 miles I come to my turn and stop under some trees. I'm feeling the heat and question my decision to pedal on. Too late; now I'm in Nowheresville.

Thankfully, after the left turn, I'm in a mostly shaded valley and the temperatures are much more pleasant. I reach Hegben Lake thirsty, so I stop at a store that isn't what I thought it was. The store's being renovated with freshly painted, bright white walls, new display cases, and is partially stocked with wine, fancy drinks, cheese, and crackers. Must be catering to folks at the resort behind the store, nothing for me.

I head outside and gaze at the lakeshore marina when a horrifying squeal of brakes startles me. I run down the road in the direction of the screech and my draw drops as I watch a truck flip over and over and down an embankment. Holy sh*t! I run back to the store and tell the woman in the doorway to call 911. Then I run 50 yards back and cross the road to where the pickup truck had come to rest, on its roof.

The truck windows are broken, and I hustle to the driver's side door. A guy's crawling out the window as I peer inside. There are two more men and I can't tell if they are conscious.

"Are you okay?" I ask them, trying to stay calm for their sake. One has blood on his face, but both are alive and breathing. A few other people have come over. The first guy out is apparently the driver because he starts yelling at a woman standing nearby.

"You cut me off! What the hell were you doing?!" He's enraged. I know he's also in shock.

"Easy," I said. "Is everyone all right? We can deal with what happened later." I position myself between the man and woman. She's mortified; he has steam coming from his ears. I'm thinking, "He's lucky to walk away from this, but boy is he fired up."

I learn that one of the two had been trying to pass the other when the truck, towing a boat no less, lost control. The posted speed limit is 70 during the day for cars, 65 at night, but I have no idea how quickly they were traveling.

The cause of the screech and squeal

Amazingly, the passengers in the truck seem relatively okay. There are no severed body parts, all are conscious, all must be in shock. I usher the driver and two passengers away from the truck. Who knows if there's spilled gasoline? By this time a crowd of locals has gathered. I don't know what else I can do. I hadn't seen what precipitated the crash, I don't want to be interviewed by the police, and knowing that ambulances are on their way, my work here is done.

I mount the orange horse and continue cycling along the beautiful Madison River. Whew.

The north-south valley meanders in and out of shade. There are non-stop scenic views of the hills and flowing water, good pavement, and few vehicles. However, I'm growing weary. It's been a heckuva day, getting close to a century ride, and with the heat and the accident, I'm feeling it. I call a place that advertises a motel and cabins, but they're full and suggest I camp in the adjacent state forest. I decline. I want to be near people.

I reach Quake Lake and its visitor center. What a crazy history. Near midnight on August 17th, 1959, a 7.5-magnitude earthquake triggered a massive landslide. Moving at 100 miles per hour, 80 million tons of rock crashed into the narrow canyon in less than a minute, blocking the Madison River and forming Earthquake Lake.

I eat another snack, check my map and see that West Fork Cabin Camp, an RV campground and fishing guide service is a few miles away. When I arrive and check in with the owner, a Michigan transplant, who shows me where I can set up my tent in the middle of a ring of RVs. I set up as close to the edge as I can. It's odd camping surrounded by RVs. Several people are sitting outside as I come and go, wave, say hello, and are friendly enough. I'm not as isolated as if I were camping in a remote forest, but one never knows what the campground social scene may bring.

BIKING, LESSONS, BLESSINGS AND BEER

I wash my clothes while in the shower and then hang them on a clothesline. Heading back to my "campsite," a couple sitting in front of their RV say hi and I notice he's wearing a Michigan State Spartans t-shirt. That's an opening if ever there was one so I walk on over. "Michigan State?" I mock accusingly. "I'm a Wolverine myself." Were we in Michigan these might be fighting words, but in the middle of Montana? We might as well be buds. I tell them about my Michigan experiences, and after standing and talking for a bit, they invite me to sit and join them for pizza and beer.

Sparty!

They're from Marquette in the Upper Peninsula of Michigan. He's a retired school superintendent who likes to talk, especially about the many lawsuits he had to deal with as superintendent and how they didn't phase him. I can't imagine. There are stories about this area and the great fishing. I enjoy the company before I go to my site for the night.

July 12, 2017
Earthquake Lake to Dillon, Montana – 115 miles

Forty more miles riding along the Madison River to start my first full day in Montana. Even though I'm in country as remote as Nebraska and Wyoming, I'm riding on a sliver of land between national forests, and I don't feel nearly as vulnerable as I did on the Plains. By mid-morning I'm out of the forest, and reach the first town of the day, Ennis, where I take a break, sit on a bench for a bit and find refreshment at a convenience store.

The south sun is starting to bake the now treeless, Montana countryside. Immediately after leaving Ennis, I come across a road project. After the flagger signals the okay, I start climbing. It's a 7-mile climb before the pass with over 2,000 feet of elevation gain. Since this is not a 50 mile stretch between towns, I wasn't that concerned about liquid. That was a mistake. I follow switchback after switchback, pretty dang steep and pretty darn hot. Most of the west has been so wide open that even with the curves, I can see the road ahead and behind. With the flaggers holding back the few cars on the road, I switchback the switchback. Turning my head often and

BIKING, LESSONS, BLESSINGS AND BEER

weaving back and forth, I use both lanes to minimize the incline. It's a bit more distance but a lot gentler.

As I think I near the top, I see a large dirt patch ahead with an unofficial scenic view. I head over for a rest. There's one vehicle in the lot, a Subaru Baja with a woman outside and a little boy in a car seat. I'm parched and after 3,000 miles, have less trouble asking, "Do you have any water?" You may think she'd be reticent, but remember, I'm a 55-year-old guy on a bike loaded with touring gear. Even as motley as I appear, I don't believe most people find me threatening. If you add the ability to speak articulately when I choose, most strangers are willing to talk with me. Either that or they feel pity.

No matter, this hippy-like millennial is kind and generous. She fetches a large mason jar full of ginger water from a cooler in the truck's bed. Oh my god, delicious. I don't want to finish it, so I have to exercise restraint.

Moments later, her husband and 4-year-old daughter appear from down the hill. As I continue to drink from the jar, Violet, the adorable little girl, goes into the car and pulls out a tall can of Pringles and gummy bears from her private stash. I love Pringles, especially the saltiness. Although not a gummy bear fan, I accept them graciously. I'm touched by her sweetness and generosity, the whole family's. It's dad's day off and they're on an outing to ride the old train in Virginia City, a restored Old West town. I feel like I drink too much of their ginger water, but they insist I don't. I found an oasis in the middle of this desert-like environment.

Ginger water, Pringles, and gummies

Revived physically and rejuvenated emotionally, I tackle the rest of the hill with gumption. After summitting, I speed down to Virginia City, and, as usual, the western slope proves to be much steeper than the east, or at least it seems to be as I'm in town in no time at all.

When I arrive in Virginia City, I look for the family's car, thinking I can get a gift for Violet, but I can't find it. There are a number of tourist spots. While taking in the town, I meet a fit looking 75- and 73-year-old Danish couple who are also crossing the country on bikes. They did the same trip 20 years ago and notice how much busier roads and parks are now. They're also heading west but have been making better time than they anticipated and are stopping here for the day. Could I do be doing this ride 20 years from now?

BIKING, LESSONS, BLESSINGS AND BEER

I take my next break at the Twin Bridges Library where I find a striking mural on the wall and two posters most interesting. One is for a Meth Watch Program and the other is advertising a program called "Get to Know Your Wildlife Neighbors: Wolverines" being held next week in Melrose. Meth and wolverines, in Montana. There's also a bikers-only campground here, but it's mid-afternoon, I'm closing in on Missoula, so I opt to motor on. The Sirens still get me every damn time.

Mural in Twin Bridges

Of course, after leaving Twin Bridges I'm baking. I know I sound like a broken record, but I typically have three choices:

1. End my riding by mid-afternoon and find a place to camp.
2. Take the afternoon off, then ride some more and find a place

to camp as dusk falls.

3. Ride through the afternoon heat.

In spite of how draining the riding it is, biking through the afternoon is almost always the winner. Thus, after 30 more miles of hard and hot riding, it's early evening when I pull into Dillon, Montana. Since Dillon is near gold mines and a railroad hub, it's maintained; a population of 4,000 people, larger than anywhere else around.

I bike into, through and out of the small city to a family-packed KOA. I check in at the office and am given a site without hookups bordering the Beaverhead River. I plug my phone into one of the unused sites with electricity and set up camp. Unlike the Madison River, there are way too many skeeters and black flies here.

I'm beat after a 120-mile day and the biting buggers are especially annoying. I get eaten alive as I set up my tent, so when a woman walks by from a nearby site, I ask if she has anything for the bugs. She tells me her husband does and points to a guy sitting behind a pick-up at a campsite beyond me.

I mosey over and let the guy know that his wife sent me over for bug repellant. He's not overly friendly but he shows me an assortment of five different bottles. I pick the one I'm familiar with and he tells me to keep it. I thank him, and noticing that his license plate is from California, I tell him that's where I'm headed. For some reason he lets me know that his brother-in-law is Clif of Clif Bar

BIKING, LESSONS, BLESSINGS AND BEER

fame. Wow.

Before I can censor myself and he can offer, I ask him if he has any bars. What happened to my humility? Maybe I'm just tired, either that or I'm getting greedy. He goes into the truck and hands me one their new bars, Sierra Trail. I thank him, never getting his name.

After cooking dinner and not wanting to hang out in this bug-infested campground, I bike a few miles to grab a beer at the the Beaverhead Brewery on the outskirts of town. It's just after 8 o'clock when I get there and they're closing. Welcome to Dillon, where the brew pub closes before dark. I'm reluctant to leave my naked bike locked outside a bar in town, so I go into one of the West's ubiquitous casino/gas station/convenience stores and buy a tomato beer. I take it to a small city park where signs let me know that alcohol is prohibited. There's no one around so I surreptitiously drink my first tomato beer out of the tall can. It's not as tasty as the one I had in Fort Collins, could have been the company. I drink half, pour out the other half, and head to Bugville, KOA to sleep.

July 14, 2017

Dillon to Sula, Montana – 103 miles

As soon as I wake, I pack and bike to town for a cup of coffee. The streets are empty in the Montana morning until I bike around the corner and standing in the middle of the road are a cow and calf.

Good moooooorning, Dillon

While Vermont has the greatest ratio of dairy cows to people, there are many more cows in Montana. Actually, there are more cows than people in Montana, beef cattle that is.

I struggle to find the right road out of town. I'm looking to get on Route 278 but the roads in town have names and not numbers. Google Maps tell me to ride I-15 but I hope this isn't right. I ride onto the overpass. Below me are cars going way too fast. I am not dealing with that. I turn around. Did I miss a turn? I cross over the interstate and see a road paralleling it. This has got to be it. I ride it for a few miles until it cuts west from the highway and then it starts to climb and climb. Seems like every time I'm climbing high and hard in Montana thinking I must be done with the steepest section, I come to a sign alerting me to a "Chain Up Area in a half-mile." And every time I see this I get bummed out because this means that I have another half-mile climb until I reach a pull out where people put chains on their cars in the winter. Then comes the really steep part, hence the need for chains. These are big-ass hills out here.

Just when you think you're at the top

Once I summit it's a beautiful descent into a gorgeous valley. Just me and ranch land for miles. Then another climb, another "Chain Up" area, and views of the Bitterroot Mountains. I'm now riding between two national forests, the Bitterroot on my left and the Beaverhead-Deerlodge on my right. These are gigantic woods, combined they're close to the size of Vermont. Cycling through a valley with no hills and omnipresent mountain views, I feel like I can ride forever.

When I reach Jackson, the only town for some time, I ought to break. I've gone 50 miles with two passes thus far this morning. The Bunkhouse Hotel is the only game in town. The former bunkhouse makes me imagine what the Old West must have been like. Luckily the post office uses the hotel lobby as the postmistress is what's keeping the place open this morning. There are muffins and coffee so I partake and leave a donation. There's even a bathroom with cloth towels.

Next, it's onto Wisdom where I only obtain lunch, no pronounced insights. I have 38 miles to get to Sula and my Warm Showers hosts. I'm now out of the sun and in the shade-filled national forest. As I pedal on the afternoon clouds start to gather and darken. I'm heading north, the clouds are coming from the west, and I'm not eager to get caught in a thunderstorm. Another conundrum. Do I accept what will come with the weather or do I bust my butt and try to beat it? With about 25 miles to go, of course I figure I can beat the storm, so I motor on. That is until I start to climb.

It's time for another pass, Chief Joseph Pass. It's a bear, steep and long. I learned and taught American Indian culture and history earlier in my career, and Chief Joseph is the author of one of my favorite quotes, "I will fight no more forever." Albeit he spoke these words after the U. S. government lied, swindled, and massacred his people. This quote always touched me, tragic for the Nez Perce and a despicable testament of U.S. genocide. As an East Coaster, this trip has opened my eyes to many things I had not previously experienced in our land. One is that as I bike through many reservations, the plight of the Native Americans moves me. Talk about people whom the U.S. has screwed over and are often ignored in today's world.

I summit the pass and what I expect to be my final crossing of the Continental Divide. I'm now astride the Idaho-Montana border in the Bitterroot Mountains. As always, after each pass comes the downhill and this one is a screamer, the most dramatic yet. With a loaded bike, I take the steep, sharp turns cautiously. There are hairpin turns galore and rocks strewn across the road. Plus, I have a loaded bike, not the most agile contraption. For 7 miles I lean on the brakes, extremely glad that they're disc brakes with better stopping power and not burning rubber like the old-style pads. I descend pretty darn slowly, no time for machismo.

The road eventually levels, my hands and arms are tired are shaky, so I stop in Sula which is all of a store, two gas pumps, and 37 people. I check my directions and look for the road to my hosts. I'm very close, and after pedaling only a mile up a dirt road, I'm there. Hallelujah.

Linda and Phil are an extremely sweet, mostly retired couple who moved to Sula several years ago from New Mexico. Phil raises goats, popular meat for new immigrants he tells me. The two came after the 350,000-acre wildfire in the summer of 2000. I explore the environs, visit the goats, and am in awe at the fire's aftermath 17 years later.

17 years later

When I return, Phil and Linda and I enjoy a delicious dinner capped with homemade peach cobbler and vanilla ice cream from their goats' milk. It's also Phil's birthday! The next morning I'll have the same ice cream in my coffee; it's out of this world.

BIKING, LESSONS, BLESSINGS AND BEER

July 15, 2017

Sula to Missoula, Montana – 90 miles

I'm in a different space early this morning as I prepare to ride out of Sula. I try to be quiet as I pack, but at 6 a.m. Linda catches me on the porch. Today I should be in Missoula and see my son Jake, a milestone of sorts. Missoula, Montana has been my fallback destination from the start. If I could bike to Montana from Vermont, I told myself and others this spring, that would be something. As soon as I started knocking off hundred-mile days, I knew that short of a physical calamity, I would make it to California. I bid Linda goodbye and hum along at a good clip down Route 93 with the snow-capped Bitterroots on my left.

I have only 80 miles of hill-less riding today, so after about 50 miles decide to take a detour at Stevenson for a bike festival that's been advertised along the trail. I figure I should support this. When I get to Stevenson there's not much to see or do at the festival yet. Of course, there's beer but it's a tad too early and hot for me to partake.

I learn the fascinating story of the Buffalo Soldiers of the 25th Infantry Regiment. Based out of Fort Missoula, they were the first U.S. troops to use bicycles. The idea was that bikes could replace horses since one doesn't have to feed a bike. The all-black regiment reached Alliance, Nebraska on July 4, 1897, covering 1,000 miles in 21 days. Their two-wheelers were fitted with steel rims, puncture-proof tires, reinforced forks, and enclosed gear cases that protected the chains. The Buffalo Soldiers climbed the Rockies, crossed the Yellowstone and Little Bighorn Rivers, and faced blinding snow on one speed, 32-pound beasts before pavement no less. And I complain about a little heat, a thunderstorm and a parched throat on my 14 speed, 22-pound bike? While the Buffalo Soldiers were successful, the start of the Spanish-American War and the advent of motorcycle followed by the invention of the automobile made bike riding troops obsolete.

Of course, it's hot by noon. I ride through ubiquitous exurban roads that border every U.S. city, but at least have easy access to shade and drinks. When I call Jake and tell him I'm 30 miles from Missoula, he tells me he's heading to meet me on his bike. Of course, that's only the plan. I ride on and see a commotion ahead. Official-looking folks are setting up a roadblock and cars are slowing down. I pass cars while riding in the shoulder until I reach the emergency crews stopping traffic and me. Uh oh. I got there minutes too late if you're a fan of real life macabre.

On my left are a few mangled vehicles, fire trucks, ambulances, and first responders' cars. An ambulance crew surrounds one of the

BIKING, LESSONS, BLESSINGS AND BEER

crash cars. It does not look good. A chopper flies in while the stopped drivers and I watch them pull the victim out of the ambulance into the helicopter. I've now been present at two crashes, both in Montana. Not long after I pass the accident, I get a flat. It's Indiana all over again. Will I ever get to Missoula? I change tubes, continue on, and soon hear, "Amos!" from across the road. Jake!

July 15 – 18, 2017

Missoula & the Mission Mountains, Montana

Jake leads us to where he's living and working, an organic farm a few miles outside town. I'll set up my tent on the edge of one of the veggie fields because Jake and his girlfriend, Cory's "home" is a single, cramped room that's part of a garlic-filled barn. It's one powerful odor; good thing they like garlic.

Later that afternoon Cory, Jake, and I leave the farm and spend a beautiful weekend hiking and camping in the Mission Mountains. The Missions are big; a dozen summits rise above 9,000 feet and a handful are visible as we do an evening hike to a waterfall. The next day we climb until we reach the base of the peaks where permanent snowfields feed sparkling tarns (glacier-formed lakes). More stunning waterfalls careen down from the higher terrain.

Made it to the farm, and Jake

A section adjacent to where we hike belongs to the Flathead Indian Reservation. In 1979, the Confederated Salish and Kootenai tribes protected almost 100,000 acres of tribal lands, making it the only tribal wilderness in the nation to be established by the actual tribe. Each summer grizzlies gather here to feast on swarms of cutworm moths and ladybugs. In order to avoid disturbing them, a good-sized chunk of the forest is off-limits from mid-July to October. Fine by me. I've thus far avoided being a meal and have no need to hike and camp in grizzly world.

Jake takes Monday off, we bike around Missoula, go tubing in the scenic and frosty Blackfoot River, enjoying cold beer and sweet riffles. Jake has to work on Tuesday, so after exploring Missoula and biking around the University of Montana campus, it's time to replace my nearly tread-bare tires.

Cory and Jake in the Mission Mountains

Jake's rear wheel is a mess, so I ride his bike to Free Cycles. The first thing I see are hundreds of old bikes outside. Inside I'm introduced to this tremendous, community bike organization. Folks come in, take an orientation course, volunteer 4 hours, and can build or fix a bike from existing bikes which they will then own. Or people can bring in their own bikes, use the tools, and get help from experts.

Kids are given bikes, and people who are homeless, in poverty, as well as others across the socio-economic spectrum benefit. What a great vibe in this action-packed, happy, 28-year-old institution. I figure the wheel just needs to be trued. Bob, the founder, whose parent coincidentally live the town south of me, takes a look and lets me know there's more to it. He tells me to see if I can find the same size wheel in the back where they have used parts galore or out back where there are hundred of more wheels and bicycles. I have no luck finding the right size wheel, so Bob gets me started. It needs four new spokes and he wants me to repack the hub.

After taking the wheel apart, repacking the hub, replacing four broken spokes, and truing the wheel as best as I can, I reinflate the tire. Boom! I guess some of the spoke nipples extend too far out of the rim. Nothing is simple when I try to fix something. I buy a new tube, pump it up, and there's no kaboom. I make a donation to Free Cycle and ride Jake's moderately improved two-wheeler home.

July 19, 2017
Missoula to Big Arm, Montana – 85 miles

Jake's working today and it's time to move on. Jake's heard that Flathead Lake, Montana's largest body of water is beautiful. Even though it will take me 80 miles north of my route, I'm well ahead of schedule so I arrange for a Warm Showers near the lake.

Arranging a homestay is an interesting proposition. Sometimes

BIKING, LESSONS, BLESSINGS AND BEER

when I email or text, hosts are away, or they don't respond. A day, several days, even weeks later I've gotten a text or email, always apologetic, that says, "Sorry to have missed you." Or, "If you are ever this way again be sure to call." "Have a great trip." Other times hosts with whom I correspond make a marketing pitch. "We'd love for you stay with us." "Let us know what you like to eat." "We can meet you in town, we can give you a lift…"

As a stranger in my own land, these Warm Showers stays and correspondences make me feel good while the hospitality can be overwhelming. I try to be as helpful a guest as I can, at the very least always clean up after myself and do dishes. I offer to help with home projects, but these are universally rejected.

I don't need much, I'm appreciative, eat anything, and am flexible and tolerant. I genuinely enjoy hearing people's stories, touring their homes, and learning about their communities. I've become a much better listener on this trip. Besides, I've found that most people like to talk. After a few days I may not be as charming, and sometimes I get tired of people's company as I'm sure they do of mine. That's another one of the benefits of this trip, I keep moving. I can be alone or with others, it's my choice. Not to toot my horn too loudly, here are reviews from some hosts with whom I have stayed:

> *"Amos was a great guest, curious, friendly and low maintenance. Epic journey for a man in his 50's. Kudos to*

you, Amos."

"Amos was a great guest at our house. He showed up with fresh veggies to add to our grill and was fun to have around. I enjoyed riding out a bit with him the next morning and helping him stay off the busier roads."

"Amos stayed for a night in Post Falls, ID, and it was a pleasure to host him! He's easygoing, open minded, and a great conversationalist. Amos is welcome to stay again any time!"

"Great visitor, great visit. Independent, resourceful, and eager to explore the people and places of our community. Three nights and two days due to a UPS delay: we were pleased for the extension of time."

"Amos is a stand up individual who delights as much in meeting the people along the way as in the biking adventure itself. Good conversation, laughs, and stories were our experience. He was able to stay with us one night and is easy to have in your home. Amos is not picky about anything - his wife of 30 years raised him well!!"

As I migrate across our country, and I imagine largely because of my excellent reviews, I sometimes have more homestay offers than I need. Who'd have thunk? It's an easy ride north on Route 93 towards

BIKING, LESSONS, BLESSINGS AND BEER

Flathead Lake. A highlight is biking through the Flathead Indian Reservation where I see signs in Salish, the native language, and bridges designed for animal crossings. When I reach the lake's south shore in Paulson, I look for good ice cream. I pass on the Dairy Queen and stop at a homemade ice cream shop, but I am discouraged by the long line. I venture off the lakeshore road into town and spot "The Cove" advertising their "Superb Montana Made Ice Cream." I'm in huckleberry country so order a scoop of chocolate and another of huckleberry ice cream. Superb indeed.

I reach Alan's home mid-afternoon and am warmly welcomed as I've always been by my Warm Showers hosts. Alan's a peach. A wee bit older than me, he's also a runner and biker. He is semi-retired and loving life. From Newburgh, NY, not far from my boyhood home, Alan moved to his sister's house when he semi-retired a few years ago.

At Flathead Lake with Alan

Our having a lot in common makes for an easy visit. We take a walk to Flatlhead Lake where I swim in delightfully refreshing water. Flathead Lake is not only Montana's biggest, it's the largest natural freshwater lake west of the Mississippi River outside of Alaska. After the walk and swim, Alan, his sister, his girlfriend, and I hang out; the ladies drink cocktails and Alan I have satisfying, local double IPAs, a marvelous dinner with another beer (one too many), and homemade cookies for dessert.

July 20, 2017

Big Arm to Thompson Falls, Montana – 81 miles

I wake up groggy from a poor night's sleep; the chocolate and two double IPAs taking their toll on this lightweight. I can't leave as early as I normally do because last night Alan started sourdough batter for his special pancakes. Being gracious, I have to eat them; not that my arm has to be twisted. This seems like the best way for me to give back to my generous hosts along with being kind, helpful, and providing sincere reviews on my hosts' profile pages.

As soon as I leave Alan's I'm ascending. Climbing at the start of a cool, new day's so much better than doing so later in the hot

BIKING, LESSONS, BLESSINGS AND BEER

afternoon, even if I am feeling out of it. I bike through an area protected for bighorn sheep, and although I continuously scan the hills, I don't see anything with four legs. I head southwest towards the Clark Fork River and hit an early headwind. This is going to be a rough day. It's been 30 miles when I come to a gas station/convenience store outside the resort town of Hot Springs. It's too hot for me to soak. After a snack and coffee, I trudge on.

A few days ago, I arranged for a possible Warm Shower in Plains, the first town I'd reach on the Clark Fork River. "Possible" because I made this contact a few days ago not knowing exactly when I'd arrive and for other reasons. I get there early; it's noon and consider my next steps.

The hosts' profile reads in part: "Please note that we are two gay men and we have four rescued Miniature Pinscher dogs, so if you are uncomfortable around gay people or household animals, you probably won't want to stay here… The household is clothing optional, but if you are uncomfortable with nudity, we promise to keep clothed during your visit…"

I read this to my daughter. "You've got to do it," she pleads. I admit, it would be different from my stays thus far. The hosts and I have exchanged a few texts. They tell me they have another person staying with them, and they want to be sure I know they have a clothing optional home. Being naked doesn't concern me at all. I haven't had an issue with nudity since my teenage days when we frequently skinny-dipped in reservoirs. But this could be odd, alone in Montana with only my bike. While far from homophobic, these are the first hosts who state their sexuality. Maybe there was more to it, maybe not. They could've had bad experiences in the past.

I deliberate. What would it be like walking around naked with a gaggle of little dogs and several gay men? I decide to take a longish lunch break in the town park where I find a seat on a bench in the shade, and fix a lunch of sardines, bread, and carrots. I'm alone in the park, one road behind the main street, when a guy pulls up in his car.

"Are you the guy staying at Bryan and Kevin's?" he asks. You have got to be kidding me. It's like the phone store in Indiana. No way I'm going incognito on this trip. It turns out that this dude is the friend staying with the naked Warm Showers hosts. How did he find me? I don't think to ask but figure he was passing by and saw my bike. He seems okay, tells me that he's from Washington and stays with these guys every summer. I deliberate some more. It's still quite early in the day and if I stay here, I'll miss out on cycling a bunch more miles. Of more concern is that I may have to be social for hours and I'm just not feeling up to it. If it were later in the day, if I felt better… I text Bryan, thank him, and tell him that I won't be staying in Plains tonight.

After rejecting Bryan and Kevin, the light southerly headwind

BIKING, LESSONS, BLESSINGS AND BEER

I've been facing all morning turns into a fierce westerly. As the temperature climbs, I'm barely moving forward. It's 25 miles to the nearest town and a bit more to the state park beyond that. At the rate I'm going, I have 3 more hours with no shade, lots of wind, no houses, and no places to stop. I'm miserable. I stop for a snack at the only shady spot I see, a trailer's driveway. It's a rundown scene and when I hear dogs barking, I decide to stay at the top of the drive, in the sun. So much for shade.

The short break doesn't revive me. I'm toast. I pedal on, ever so slowly. When I reach the first intersection I've come to in miles, I stop. There is no one and no thing around, just the entrance to a logging company on my left. My tank is empty. The wind, heat, and hangover have drained me. I lay my head on my forearms and rest on my handlebars. I'm convinced it's karma sinking its teeth into my arse for rejecting my hosts in Plains.

A truck that had passed earlier stops along side of me. Woo hoo!

"Are you okay?" the driver asks through an open window.

"I'm fine, just beat," I say, hoping to God he offers me a ride. I don't give a rat's ass if it's considered cheating. Besides, cheating according to whom?

"It's only 5 miles to town," he tells me, encouragingly. Only? I so badly want to ask for a ride, but I can't. What would I say? "Excuse me, Sir. I know that I've ridden 3,000 miles and it's 5 more miles to town, but there's just no way I can make it. Would you mind giving me a lift?"

He doesn't offer a ride and makes a left turn. Oh well, at least he wasn't going my way. Five painstakingly slow miles later I make it to the outskirts of Thompson Falls and stop at a Subway to enjoy the ice from their soda machine. It's a challenge to fill the Camelback with ice and I make a mess as I often do; I probably should use a cup. An old-timer watching from a nearby booth grumbles, "I hope you clean that up." I suppose he's right, so I go to the counter and ask for a towel. The woman working tells me not to worry about it. Nodding in the direction of the curmudgeon she says, "He's a grumpy old fart."

Mildly restored, I carry on to Thompson Falls State Park a few miles further west. It's early evening when I pull in and am greeted by the campground hostess outside of her trailer.

"We're full," she tells me. What?! "But, as a biker," she continues, "You're entitled to the picnic area, the best spot in the park." I follow her and her golf cart. She's right. It is a stunning site overlooking the river. I set up camp and head down to the water. I go to a sandy spot where I undress and take a sensational, refreshing, calming dip in the Clark Fork. I walk for a ways in both directions, but not too far—my body is tired. There's been little walking this summer. I cook dinner overlooking the Clark Fork River loving the views and tranquility. After a wicked hard day, I'm content. The story of my trip, joy to

BIKING, LESSONS, BLESSINGS AND BEER

misery, misery to joy.

July 21, 2017

Thompson Falls, Montana to Clark Fork, Idaho – 60 miles

I awake rested after a calm night in a beautiful setting. In several hours I'll be in Idaho, state number twelve. It should be an easy day today, only 60 miles to Clark Fork where I have two Warm Shower offers. One's from a restaurant owner who tells me I'm welcome to stay at her home. She'll be working, has other guests, and is still glad to host me. My other offer is from Spencer whose profile reads,

> *Katherine and I own and operate an organic vegetable farm in Clark Fork, Idaho. When we aren't farming, we are avid cyclists, both touring and road riding. We've used Warm Showers extensively as guests when we are on our own trips, and we want to keep the hospitality rolling forward as hosts. Stop by for a shower, a place to sleep, and meals!*

While the restaurant owner sounds great, Katherine and Spencer sound even better. As anticipated, the ride into Idaho is chill. No mountain passes, little traffic, and no navigation as I stay on Route 200 with the Clark Fork River on my left. It's a gorgeous, sunny day with no headwind and I'm in no hurry. As if things cannot get better, I come to another major road construction project giving me miles of the road to myself.

When I get to Noxon, population 218, I take a detour to the other side of the river. There's a small store where I enjoy a snack and try to phone to confirm that I will indeed be at Spencer and Katherine's later today. I have no cell service and the woman behind the counter lets me use her phone.

It's early afternoon when I reach the town of Clark Fork, population 536, and spot Clark Fork Pantry on the other side of the road. A few bikes are parked outside, and people are eating on the deck. I ride over, lock up my bike and am greeted by the folks dressed in bike gear.

"How's the food?" I wonder.

"Delicious."

They ask about my trek, and hearing out I'm from Vermont, one of the bikers says, "I have a brother-in-law who farms in Vermont."

"Where?" I ask.

"Thetford." That's where we used to live and only 10 miles up the road from where we now live. Jeannie loves his tomatoes. A non-biking woman chimes in. "I have a cousin in Vermont."

"Where?"

"Tunbridge," she answers. She's got to be kidding. "What's her name?"

Of course I know her cousin and her cousin's kids. The boy was

BIKING, LESSONS, BLESSINGS AND BEER

a student of mine years ago in a school where I was principal. Crazy. She informs me that Josh will be a high school senior this year. I tell her to send my regards.

What are the odds? It's not like Vermont is that small. There are over 600,000 of us and I'm in friggin' Idaho.

After eating a Reuben sandwich and with time to pass before heading to my hosts, I ride around the area, enjoy the spectacular mountain views, ride along fields, cross the river, and visit the library. It's a joy to have a beautiful day and to have reached my destination in the afternoon. No Sirens haunt me today.

Before riding the 3 miles to my hosts, I stop by the Squeeze Inn Restaurant whose owner is the other potential Warm Showers host. I ask a woman setting tables outside if Janet's here. She's Janet's daughter and Janet's not here yet, so I ask her to thank her mom and let her know I have another place to stay.

As the afternoon grows late, I head out of town and make a right up a narrow river valley. While Spencer offered to meet me in town, I have no problem biking a few miles up a dirt road. Compared to Nebraska sand, Idaho dirt is a pleasure. After I head down a long driveway I'm welcomed by Katherine and Spencer who're wrapping up preparations for tomorrow's farmer's market. I ask what I can do, and other than move a few boxes, they're all set.

Although much younger than me, I instantly feel a connection.

They're modern day back-to-the-landers, living simply and simply living. The two of them built a very small home, do not yet have running water, and have an impressive greenhouse and vegetable plots. The land belongs to Spencer's dad who had homesteaded part-time in the '70s. Spencer and Katherine are in it whole hog, full-time. Spencer's from Portland, Katherine's from Seattle, and they met in Maine after college.

Spencer gives me a tour and shows me the bathroom and warm shower outdoors at the edge of the woods. The shower uses a bucket with water warmed by the sun and feels amazing on a warm afternoon. I take in the scenic views from atop the toilet. Spencer and Katherine are living like I had decades ago, albeit for a much shorter time. They're smart, hard-working, and generous. It's the most primitive home I have stayed in during my travels and I love it, at least in the summer. They tell me not to be fooled. The Idaho panhandle is sun-rich now but cloudy most of the year.

BIKING, LESSONS, BLESSINGS AND BEER

Katherine and Spencer in Clark Fork

Spencer and I make a run to the feed store and afterwards they indulge me in a hearty, homemade dinner. They want me to sleep in their loft as they prefer the tent. After dinner we sit by a fire while enjoying the setting sun and cooler temperatures. They are the youngest folks to host me, and I realize I've made friends and stayed with people in nearly every decade of adult life, from those in their twenties to octogenarians.

Idaho

July 22, 2017

Clark Fork to Sagle, Idaho – 40 miles

Today, Moose Meadow Organics, aka Katherine and Spencer, will set up a stand at the weekly farmer's market in Sandpoint, the biggest city around and just 60 miles south of the Canadian border. Before I head off, I ask if there is anything I can do to help, but other than loading some things into the truck, they're set. I head off to Sandpoint on Caballo Naranjo planning to meet them at the market. Spencer passes me on the way in his pick-up and waves. It's about a 30-mile ride and another beautiful day. The road is a bit more crowded, but the speed limit is relatively low.

BIKING, LESSONS, BLESSINGS AND BEER

In a few hours I meet Spencer and Katherine at the bustling market. There are others selling veggies, but most are food vendors and crafts. Katherine goes off to deliver vegetables to restaurants and I work the booth while Spencer gets change from the bank.

I love that he trusts me with his cash box and veggie stand. It reminds of when I was at a conference in New Orleans and a woman asked me to watch her jewelry stand for the same reason, only I just met her. I must give off a trustworthy vibe. When Spencer returns, I mosey around the green for a while and then bid Spencer farewell; I have a date at noon with my next hosts.

Before my trip my brother and I tried to figure out a place where he could join me for part of the ride. We didn't solidify the plan until a few weeks ago when we decided he'd meet me in Spokane, Washington. Steve wants to ride with me but is conflicted. He's concerned that he might mess with my mojo. I tell him not to worry, every day is a different trip. Heck, every day is multiple trips. I know his company will be tremendous and add new twists and turns. We plan to ride together to Eugene, Oregon where he'll fly home and I'll continue south.

I have plenty of time to get to Spokane, so I've been slowing down and plan to keep doing so, enjoying the Warm Showers hosts. My homestay tonight is in Sagle, only 10 miles south of Sandpoint. I get a message from my hosts, Julie and Rick, that they're having lunch in town with East Coast friends, Paul and Karen, and invite me to meet them. I ride to the restaurant where Paul treats me to a delicious lunch outdoors. Afterwards they're heading out on their motor boat and invite me to join, another way to see Idaho. Rick suggests we go to his local bike shop to leave my bike and gear for safe-keeping, another benefit of local connections.

We do and then walk to the public boat launch at Lake Pend Oreille ("ear hanging" in French as some explorers thought this is the lake's shape), the largest lake in Idaho. The views and shoreline are beautiful, especially with the deep blue skies overhead. The lake's over 1,000 feet deep in places, and because of the Japanese attack on Pearl Harbor during World War II, the south end was the second largest naval training ground in the world and the largest "city" in the state. It's still used by the Navy to test submarines.

We spend several hours on the boat swimming, touring the lake, enjoying beer and each others' company. Rick's an elementary school teacher, Julie's a physical therapist, Paul's a doctor, and Karen's a nurse; they have kids close to the ages of mine and are probably the hosts most similar to me. Late in the afternoon they drop me off at the boat launch; they'll motor closer to their home and I'll bike there.

BIKING, LESSONS, BLESSINGS AND BEER

On Lake Pend Oreille with Julie, Rick, Karen, and Paul

Caballo Naranjo's still at the shop when I return although bike dude teases that it tempted him to go for a spin. I head to Sagle, and of course it being the end of the day, it's a hilly and hard ride. I don't mind when I have my first lengthy train delay, about 5 minutes waiting for an endless freight train to pass. I'm welcomed at Julie and Rick's, given a room, and take a shower. We eat a delicious cookout of steak and veggies I brought from the farmers market.

After dinner we play my first ever frisbee-drinking game. Julie puts a beer bottle on each of two posts about 20 yards apart. The object is for one team to knock down the other team's bottle. You can't stand in front of the bottle but can catch the bottle if it falls or you reach out to catch the frisbee before it hits the bottle or post. Points are awarded depending if you drop a catchable frisbee, the bottle falls to the ground, or the frisbee hits the post. All the while you're holding your beer. Obviously, the game gets progressively more challenging the more we drink.

This is so cool. I met these folks today and am now playing drinking games in their yard. I boated, dined, talked, drank, played, and am spending the night in the home of these new friends I just met.

July 23, 2017
Sagle to Post Falls, Idaho – 70 miles

After coffee this morning, I experience another first. Rick and Paul accompany me towards Post Falls where I'll be staying tonight. This is a real treat. I don't have to think about navigation, we avoid main roads and I have great company. We ride through quiet, scenic countryside for 20 miles before they head back.

With plenty of time before I'm due at my next Warm Showers this evening, I toodle on to explore Coeur d'Alene, 10 miles east of my route. I pass a bank with balloons outside and see people coming and going. They're having an open house and I enjoy cake and get a free toothbrush. Next, I come to a bike store where they're offering a bike safety rodeo for young ones. With all the time I want, I stop and observe. It's on to the Idaho Centennial Trail paralleling Interstate 95.

BIKING, LESSONS, BLESSINGS AND BEER

After a few miles I come to a highway rest area and I stop just to do so. It's odd pulling into a highway rest area on a bicycle.

When I get to Coeur d'Alene, I see signs for a big band concert in the park, so I listen for a while. The heat from the pavement and cars make the city especially hot, so it's time for the usual afternoon indulgence: ice cream. I find a store with locally made ice cream and it is scrumptious. As I unlock my bike, a guy and gal approach me. He asks how I am, tells me that he used to work in a bike shop in Spokane, gives me his number and tells me to call if I need anything while in Spokane. At this point of my trip, this seems normal. I'm still grateful and appreciative. I've been blessed, repeatedly.

It's only late afternoon and I'm not due at my host's for a while so I decide to pedal along the smooth bike lane long the northern shore of Lake Coeur d'Alene. I know it sounds crazy to bike for "fun" with all the bicycling I'm doing, but this is a mad summer and the two wheels are my means of travel and exploration. Cycling along the fairly flat lakeshore with warm temps and a breeze is a great way to sightsee, even if I am going out and back. When I've had enough of the lake, I turn back towards the city and encounter a bunch of bikes parked outside a lakeside bar. I'm in no hurry so I stop and greet the bikers sitting at the table.

"Mind if I join you?"

"If you think you can hack it," one calls out.

I laugh. "I think so. I biked here from Vermont." That's enough for them to "Ooooh" and "Ahhhh" and insist on treating me to a beer. Apparently two people ordered, or the waiter also treated as two of Washington's finest bottles appear in front of me. It's been a hot day and I have no problem enjoying both. The group's on a mellow (20 to 40 miles a day), supported tour on the bikeways of the region.

The cycling god

To them I am a god. I assure them that I'm a mere mortal, just like them. I push down on my pedals and shift my gears the same way they do. No matter how much I tell them what they're doing's fantastic, it's all about biking your ride, and the biggest difference is that I devoted more time to training and riding, they won't have it. I'm a living legend. They're folks who have come from all over the

BIKING, LESSONS, BLESSINGS AND BEER

country for this trip. It's fun sharing stories, laughing, and drinking with them. When it's time to say goodbye, I don't mind that I have another 10 miles, they're done for the day and that I'll be continuing, self-supported and alone, at least until tomorrow.

I leisurely bike to Post Falls with a slight buzz, no hurry, enjoying the surroundings until the last 2 miles when I must climb an enormous hill overlooking the city. I find the house and I'm welcomed by my host, Jim. If you think I'm on an adventure, imagine what my new host Jim and his brother did. They biked through the U.S. and Asia for 3 years. Three years! They stopped for months at a time to work. Jim's odyssey continued for 3 years, 2 and a half for his brother, who eventually ran out of money.

As Jim and I get to know one another, he lets me know that he's preparing to move to Thailand. He lives in this house belonging to his friend, Rob, who joins us. Rob is a wild outdoorsman. They tell me about their adventures, not bragging but incredibly entertaining. A couple knocks on the door; they're here to look at this house that's for sale. Get out. I'm being hosted by a man who's living in a friend's house who's preparing to move to Thailand, and the house is currently being shown to sell. Still they put me up. Talk about generosity. *It's always a mitzvah (good deed) to share your home with strangers.*

Jim asks if I like Thai food. I love it. Jim and I talk as he prepares and cooks what sure tastes like an authentic Thai dinner: delicious, flavorful, and spicy accompanied by an Idaho brew. He's a mellow, engaging dude and I would've enjoyed hanging a little longer, but Li'l Stevie's arriving the next day in Spokane and I've got to get there.

Washington & Oregon

July 24, 2017

Post Falls, Idaho to Ritzville, Washington – 100 miles

I ride the Centennial Trail which alternating between a gorgeous bike trail along the Spokane River, a path adjacent to the highway, and a road through neighborhoods. I reach Spokane late in the morning and my brother's due early afternoon. We're meeting at the Bike Hub where Steve had his bike shipped. Steve's plane's delayed and I have the guys assemble the bike, so we'll be ready to roll when he arrives.

It's going to be great hanging, riding, and sharing the journey this week with my little brother. We've done other trips together and

I'm psyched for his companionship. We're quite compatible and travel well, plus we're not too pressed to cover miles since he has two options: fly back to California from Portland or leave from Eugene, depending on how we do mileage-wise. When Steve arrives, he gears up and off we go.

I may sound like an advertisement but navigating without Adventure Cycling maps takes a heckuva lot of effort. I looked in Spokane for maps, but even the visitor bureau has nothing, and no one at the bike shop has a clue about biking where we're headed. Steve and I know we're going southwest to Portland and want to get to the Columbia River. Other than that, we'll hope for the best.

We ride the Fish Lake Trail and local roads out of Spokane. It's hot, very much so, but at least it's a dry heat. People back east (yours truly among them before this jaunt) laugh at the notion of dry heat, but it's light years better than less heat with humidity. Our first stop is for a cold drink and snack break in Cheney, the only town around, and home to University of Eastern Washington.

Temporarily resuscitated we march on, feeling pretty good when we decide to stop for dinner in Sprague. There's one place open on the main drag, the Oasis Bar & Restaurant. The joint is quiet: Steve, me, a few highway construction workers, and a couple of locals. The owner comes over to our table and begins talking local politics. He tells us that the current mayor had blocked him from getting a liquor

BIKING, LESSONS, BLESSINGS AND BEER

license so now he's running against him. He just reopened the Oasis, and he is itching for a fight. Posters announcing his candidacy hang in storefronts.

We enjoy a bottle of beer. We have to since Mr. Oasis and Sprague mayor hopeful just got his liquor license, not that you have to twist our arms. It's early evening when we finish our meal. We've put in 45 miles this afternoon and I rode 30 this morning, but we don't want to stay in Sprague. There's still light, Sprague is a dump, we'd like to get to Portland and eventually Eugene, and we're "behind" due to Steve's delayed flight. Riding out of Sprague in the cool evening air is delightful, novel, and there's almost no one on the road. Suddenly the pavement ends, the construction starts. We'd seen the signs and the workers and figured there could be a rough patch. The pavement's torn up and we ride on a black, sandy, gravel surface. It isn't great, but it's no Nebraska sand and I manage just fine with my tires, but it's hard for Steve on his thinner tires. With no one else on the road, we ride side by side, slowly. On this straight highway we can see and hear any approaching vehicles with plenty of warning.

"This sucks," we agree. Soon I'm way ahead of Steve, alone in the barren, desert-like landscape. I wait for him, watching him approach and hear the music of Bruce:

"Who's that down at the end of the alley, she's been gone so long,
Here she comes, here she comes, here she comes,

Kitty's back in town, here she comes now, Kitty's back in town..."

Steve on the black sands outside Sprague

"Can't be too much longer," we say hoping to reassure ourselves since we have no idea when the construction will end. There are no alternatives, just this one road. Soon, I'm way ahead again with no sign of pavement and we keep on, straight in the fading light. The construction project continues for 10 miles until we reach the interstate. Crossing over the highway we aim for Ritzville.

The sun is setting so we turn on our lights and cruise down the shoulder on smooth pavement. I tuck behind Steve who's absolutely flying. There's no wind, and we're humming along at 20 miles per hour, motivated by both the darkness and the desire to be done for the day.

I remember back to one Sunday when we were kids. Steve and I had gone biking around the high school. As we headed home, I zoomed down the hill until I had to slow down for the gate that closed the road on weekends. I waited on the other side of the fenced gate for Steve to catch up. I watched him cruise towards me, the gate between us. "I can't stop!" Steve screamed.

"Use your brakes!" I yelled. Crash! He careened off the fence like a baseball off a pitchback and landed on the pavement. I ran over. Steve was dazed, some scratches, but otherwise unscathed. My little brother was tough. There was also the time we were boxing in the basement. I fought from my knees to level the playing field. I landed a jab to the side of his head. He collapsed. And he didn't get up. He was seven, I was almost 12 and I thought he was dead. I killed my brother. Turns out I had only knocked him unconscious for a minute. "Don't tell Mom," I begged. He didn't.

When we reach the lights of Ritzville, we encounter a plethora of cheap motels and my brother wants to use Yelp to review them. I tell him there's no point, we're just crashing for the night and will be up and out at dawn. We choose the Empire Motel, an establishment that doesn't seem to have seen any upgrades since the 1950s. With two beds and a shower, it'll be perfect, until we can't get the shower to work. Great. The manager comes over and shows us how to work the funky mechanism to turn on the water and we wash off the layers of dirt accumulated from the torn-up pavement. Beat, I'm eager to go to bed for a fitful sleep.

One problem when arriving somewhere at night is not knowing the surroundings. I'm fast asleep in our motel room when I'm jolted awake. I jump up in my bed in a panic. I hear a freight train running right through our room. The train whistle's blowing, the locomotive is rumbling, vibrations are getting louder and its bearing down on me. Holy Sh*t! The room's shaking and the noise is so loud it feels like I'm laying on the tracks. Of course, I'm not. The train tracks are right behind our room, just feet away. Twice more I am startled out of my sleep by a freight train. Needless to say, I don't get much rest. In the morning I ask Steve how he slept. "Great," he says showing me his earplugs. *Yelp and earplugs, who'd have thunk?*

July 25, 2017

Riztville to Kennewick, Washington – 102 miles

We spend today riding rural eastern Washington. Bland is the best way to describe the desolate landscape. The highlight may be a fruit stand off the interstate where a high schooler wearing a Mets baseball cap is the lone employee. Steve and I are both Mets fans from way back, so we tell him stories of the wonder years of Shea Stadium and the three of us ponder the team's future prospects. He's a good guy, a big kid who pitches, plays first base, and loves baseball. He lets us sample ripe melons and we buy as much delicious and juicy fruit as we can eat.

Our next stop enroute to the Columbia River is Tri-city number one, Pasco at the confluence of the Yakima and Columbia Rivers. We get there at 5 p.m., it's 103 degrees and Steve thinks we should cross the Yakima and ride into Oregon. It's hard to say for sure with our lousy maps and Google, and when we get to the bridge crossing the river, we realize we messed up and rode several miles out of our way. Back we go, but first we've got to stand in the scorching sun for 10 minutes, delayed by a stopped freight train. We really need a break and have our second highlight of the day, turning Steve onto the joys of McDonalds. On this sojourn I've discovered the wonders of the air conditioning, soda fountains, and free wifi that Mickey D's offers.

We relish ice cream and A/C and then it's off to Kennewick, Tri-city number two. When we arrive at the massive blight in "Anywhere USA" with its big box stores, shopping centers, and motels near the interstate, Steve is done. We crash in an upscale motel thanks to brother Steven.

July 26, 2017

Kennewick, Washington to Hood River, Oregon – 80 miles

We have an even more remote haul planned today so we rise early. Our morning begins with a climb and an added bonus of an early morning headwind, an omen of things to come. The landscape is lunar-like with not much more than dirt surrounding us. After an hour ascending, we summit and bomb down to the Columbia River, a heckuva 30-mile warm up. We're stoked; the Columbia has a reputation for beautiful cycling. We get our bearings at the intersection with Route 14 and prepare to head west up the Washington side of the river. That is, until we see the state highway sign saying, "Next Services 83 Miles." Uh oh, that is a long way. As we peruse the map for options, a guy in a service truck pulls over.

"Do you guys need help?" he asks.

"Maybe. We heard it was sweet riding along the Columbia River, but 83 miles seems like a long stretch."

"I do some riding around here," he says. "You could ride over to the Oregon side," and he points to a trail that runs along the river. "There are trails over there."

"Great. Thanks."

We cross the Colombia into Umatilla, Oregon, my 13th state,

BIKING, LESSONS, BLESSINGS AND BEER

but I'm not in a celebratory mood. Google bike maps tells us to turn around and take Washington's Route 14 while the state map shows a patchwork of roads that parallel the Columbia River on the Oregon side. We're confused. We stop at a truck stop for drinks and to check maps, and as we get back on our bikes discover Steve has a flat. I change his tube, then we struggle getting the coin operated pump to work.

Eventually we put in more than our share of quarters and off we go, west in Oregon. This is already turning out to be quite a day and it's still early morning. The Google bike map again tells us to return to Washington. We ignore it. I'm still mad from the Nebraska sand, so we cycle Oregon back roads and state highways for two hours, often paralleling the river, until we arrive in Boardman. Armed with only Google and a state highway map that is not guiding us very well, Steve suggests we stop at the library ahead. He goes in and borrows a gazetteer while I fix a flat.

Uh oh. The gazetteer does not paint a pretty picture. We don't see anymore backroads on the maps. We're at the intersection with I-84 and it's 60 miles on the interstate to Biggs Junction, the next bridge that crosses the Columbia River. So much for the advice of that guy we met when we first reached the Columbia. I don't think he intentionally steered us wrong, but if not, he must not ride much around here. Is there a lesson? It can't be: *Don't trust strangers*. My whole trip has been in their hands. *Trust Google bike maps?* They've steered me wrong plenty of times. *Keep the faith.*

The librarian suggests we go to the Boardman Chamber of Commerce and Tourist Bureau a few miles away. She remembers sending other bikers that way once upon a time. Sounds like our best bet so we go a few miles off route, as if we have a route. The two kind ladies at the chamber of commerce pore over maps with us. They're racking their brains trying to help. Eventually we all come up with the same three options.

How to cross the river: Boardman Visitor Bureau

Option 1: Backtrack. Reverse directions and ride the 20 miles from where we came. This equates to our biking 40 hot miles with zero sum gain toward our goal of Portland. Plus, we'd still have the 83 miles to Biggs Junction with no services before then. It's now afternoon meaning we have the sun, heat and wind to contend with.

BIKING, LESSONS, BLESSINGS AND BEER

Maybe if we were retracing our route through the Tetons or Yellowstone, heck even the Adirondacks, it wouldn't be so bad. But a hazy, barren eastern Washington landscape? Twice? A miserable prospect.

Option 2: Head south on smaller roads and zigzag until we get to Biggs Junction. This would be a challenging route to create and follow. Road signage is inconsistent on the back roads and the ladies have no idea which roads to take or which roads are bikeable. Not to mention, we have no clue which roads dead end and how many times we would get lost. This also would add significant miles. On the plus side, we wouldn't be backtracking, we wouldn't have an 84-mile empty stretch and we'd avoid the interstate.

Option 3: Spend 5 hours riding I-84. This scares us. I'm the only one with interstate biking experience, a whopping half-hour in Wyoming. Steve's an interstate virgin and 60 miles is a lot of interstate cycling.

So those are our choices. Or are they? In Boardman I noticed signs to a marina and we're not far above the Columbia River. I ask the women if they think we can go to the marina and find someone to ferry us across. Better, they say, they know a fishing guide. One calls Bryce. We can hear that he's answered the phone. Our chamber of commerce friend tells us that Bryce has finished guiding for the day, he's still at the marina, and he's game. I could have hugged these two ladies. After several flats, crappy riding, and much confusion, a ferry awaits. How fortunes change. We offer our profuse thanks and are off.

Steve and I cycle downhill to the river, turn left, and on our right is the entrance to Boardman Marina and RV Park. We're feeling much more hopeful as we ride towards the marina scanning for a stranger. Moments later we see a guy emerge from a boat and onto the docks. "Bryce?" I call out from where Steve and I stand on the grass. He gives a wave. Anyone witnessing my exuberance would think he's a long-lost friend. Steve and I set our bikes down and hustle to the dock. Bryce is ready and willing to take us across the river. Of course, we tell him, we'll pay him for his efforts. As we load our bikes into his speed boat he says, "I can take you a little ways up the river. There's a state boat launch on Whitcomb Island."

"Is there a bridge?" I ask. I don't want to get stranded on that island. Of course there is. Duh. Bryce becomes our very own Charon, the ferryman from Greek mythology. Instead of carrying two newly deceased souls across the river Styx separating the world of the living from the world of the dead, Bryce ferries two *nearly* deceased bodies across the Columbia River separating Washington from Oregon.

BIKING, LESSONS, BLESSINGS AND BEER

Bryce

We load our bikes into Bryce's boat, a 2014 24-foot Umpqua Marine sled, "equipped with padded seats and armrests for a pleasurable ride." We don't relax in the padded seats as we have to make sure our bikes don't end up in the river. We motor up and across the river, our bikes balanced in the open rig, the wind keeping us cool. This is the biking life. Steve and I are tempted to ask him to keep going west. We're flying, it's too loud to have a conversation, and all we can do is smile.

After 15 minutes of zipping through the water, Bryce cuts the motor and I see the approaching boat ramp. As soon as our pace slows, we're roasting in the inferno. We express our sincere gratitude to Bryce; he saved our assess from added misery. Steve gives him money; "Share the wealth," is my brother's motto. We watch Bryce motor away and figure out our next move.

Walking our bikes up to the fish cleaning station, I look for the park's exit and a place to drink before heading out. There's one other person here, a guy getting ready to go fishing. Without my asking, he tosses me a few cold water bottles from his cooler. More acts of kindness.

Steve and I bike off Whitcomb Island, the glow from the motorboat ride now a memory. In minute we're back on Washington Highway 14, 5 hours, three flat tires, a stop at a library, a tourist bureau, prompts from Google Maps to turn around, and a boat ride across the Columbia River late, we've advanced 22 miles west from where we were at 9 a.m. We're on the same desolate state highway we started on, one lane in each direction, no shoulder, little traffic, no signs of human dwellings and "only" 61 miles to the next services. This is certainly no better than the 83 miles we had hoped to avoid. It's worse. We're tired and it's hotter.

There's only one option, head west on Highway 14. As we ride it gets hotter and windier. There's no shade. When I say no shade, I don't mean a tree here or a building there, nada. To our left is the Columbia whose bank is lined with shrubby vegetation, and to the right are charred, rocky, dirt hills. Mile after mile the terrain stays the same. I'm whipped, Steve a little less so. We try drafting off one another but I have trouble staying with him. He's traveling lighter, with a faster bike, and more energy. I ride on his tail for a bit and

BIKING, LESSONS, BLESSINGS AND BEER

then fall back. After he notices, he waits, I catch up, draft for a while, and then fall back again. With 60, 55, 50, then 45 miles to go to Biggs Junction, I'm as hurting as I have been on the trip. It's slow going, the heat and wind sapping the little energy I have. We have no choice but to continue.

There's nobody else to interact with so when we see a forest ranger and her truck on the side of the road, we stop. The ranger tells us she's looking for hot spots. The hill recently burned and observing more closely, we see embers and smoke on parts of the hillside close to us.

Hot spot

We ride on and I contemplate options. I've been in contact with a Warm Showers host named Clint who lives in Hood River, Oregon. I thought we might get there today, but with our late start from Spokane the other day and the detours today, it's not going to happen. I remember that this guy was kind in his texts; he told me to let him know if I needed anything. Okay, Clint, I need something. Let's see what you've got.

I call Clint and tell him where I think we are, near Moona, Washington. I'm not sure why Moona even has a name. Maybe there was once something here other than this lunar landscape but not now. We're in the middle of nowhere, the temperature's in the 90s, and we're cooking on the pavement. Clint answers my call and tells me he knows the area well since he's windsurfed around here. There may be camping and a store up ahead at Roosevelt Recreation Area. Sometimes it's open, other times not. He suggests we head there. It's still a ways but the best option thus far. Then, as if Moses strikes a stone to get us water in this parched earth, I hear an angel sing, a miracle in the desert. It's Clint.

"My wife's out of town… I'll come get you… I have a truck. I'll meet you at the boat launch… It'll take me an hour and a half…" I don't hear the rest of his words.

What? I'm not sure I heard him correctly. Thinking I may be delirious from the heat, I ask him to repeat what he just said. Yes, he will meet us at Roosevelt Recreation Area. Steve and I are stoked.

The good news doesn't make me pedal any faster as we creep along the Columbia for 7 more miles to Roosevelt. Still, it's a helluva lot better than 37. We get to Roosevelt, the store's open, the campground's still here. But neither matters. Clint is coming. Steve and I chow down at the store. Finally, after pedaling along the river,

BIKING, LESSONS, BLESSINGS AND BEER

biking over the river, being ferried across the river, we go down to the water with the sounds of the Talking Heads reverberating in my ears,

"Take me to the river, drop me in the water.

Take me to the river, dip me in the water.

Washing me down, washing me down."

We are finally baptized in the Columbia River, swimming in its cool waters. Our guardian angel Clint appears, we load the bikes and panniers into his truck, and begin to get to know our new friend on the ride to Hood River. Like Jim in Iowa City, we hit if off immediately. Sometimes the water flows like wine.

As we drive, we learn about the life of Clint. Married and without children, Clint tells us he likes to play. A former contractor, physical therapist, competitive windsurfer and an avid biker too, he moved here years ago for the windsurfing. Clint reveals that he is a bit chunkier than he'd like to be; we soon find out why. His wife, a friend, and he are partners in a bakery and Italian restaurant. Clint asks if we'd like to eat there tonight. Is he kidding? He doesn't have to ask.

Since we swam and changed, we go right to the Pine Street Kitchen restaurant and are seated at a table outside. We feast on fresh bread, local beer, quattro formaggio, housemade agnolotti, homemade pasta, and hot-skillet-baked brownie for dessert. The food, company, and setting are all appreciated beyond belief.

Mind you, this morning began with a hellacious climb, we then cycled on the wrong side of the river, were ferried across the river, and biked in a literal inferno while riding against fierce headwinds in 90-degree temperatures past smoldering wildfires. As has often been the case, what started out as a memorable day with its intense challenges, ends up being a monumental day due to the generosity of new friends. So many lessons: Ask for help. As much as you need. Stay positive.

Pine Street Kitchen with Clint and Steve

July 27, 2017

Hood River Area, Oregon

Steven and I camp in Clint's yard and I hardly sleep. I didn't set up a tent, and in spite of a restless night with incredible winds (there's a reason Hood River is a windsurfing mecca), we want to stick

BIKING, LESSONS, BLESSINGS AND BEER

around. Our next day of riding will take us to Portland and riding back to The Dalles, the section we missed on account of Clint's chauffeuring us, is much more appealing, as is a mellow day. Besides, Clint likes having us around and we like him. He works when he wants and is enthusiastic about taking us on a scenic bike ride. The ride does not disappoint. Views of Mt. Hood, Mt. Adams, and the Columbia River are breathtaking.

The Columbia River

Eventually Clint leaves us, and we head down to The Dalles, the next town east. Instead of biking back to Clint's and into the Hood River wind tunnel, we load our bikes on the front of a bus to take us back. In the afternoon I keep biking around Hood River; I just can't get enough of the views of Mt. Hood and Mt. Adams.

A motorboat, a pick-up truck, and now a bus. I'm still biking cross-country, aren't I?

July 28, 2017

Hood River to Portland, Oregon – 85 miles

I wake early, enjoy the surroundings, and wait for Cliff to wake. We eat breakfast together, not worried about the heat or a late start. We have only 80 mostly flat miles to ride and the temperature isn't supposed to get that high. Instead, we're a tad anxious about a different obstacle, starting the day riding 14 miles on Interstate 84, the recommended bike route. Steve's a virgin to the interstate, and I'm an experienced veteran with all of the one experience under my belt.

I-84 turns out to be fine. It's a curvy stretch of highway, more cars than I had on I-80 in Wyoming, but thankfully uneventful. Our comfort level is aided by the wide shoulder, but we're still relieved when we reach the exit at Wyeth. I can do without interstate biking and this ought to be my last stretch. We meander on and off a bike route paralleling the Colombia for the remainder of the morning. At Crown Point, a basalt promontory overlooking the river, we have lunch, chill, and chat with another guy in Mets garb as we take in the vistas.

By early afternoon we're in the Portland suburbs and all that this entails: traffic lights, sharing the road with more vehicles, noise, but

BIKING, LESSONS, BLESSINGS AND BEER

no worries. Steve wants to fully inflate his tire after we changed a flat earlier in the day, and I want to go to a marijuana dispensary. In Gresham we stop at a McDonald's for drinks, and then I go to the pot shop next store while Steve guards the bikes. Legal marijuana sold in a store. It's hard for a child of the '70s to imagine this is real. Even though Oregon's been doing this for 3 years, it's brand-spanking new and surreal to me.

Saturday afternoon and the place is hopping. After showing the woman at the entrance my passport with its photo I.D. (another stroke of luck that I both brought it and didn't lose it in Nebraska), she directs me to a giant room behind closed doors. There are display cases on the floor and wall cases like you'd find in a jewelry store. I get in line with a representative slice of America: immediately ahead of me is a caucasian woman who looks to be 10 years older than me, behind me are younger white and black men and women, folks who look like they are regulars, folks who have physical impairments, and stoner-types. When it's my turn at the display case, a man behind the counter greets me.

"How can I help you?" he cheerfully calls. "I'm Carl and I'll be your budtender." My own budtender. Carl looks to be about 30, is shorter than me and built.

"This is my first time here, and I gotta tell you, it's been a while since I've indulged."

"Are you interested in edibles or bud?" he wants to know.

I look at the enormous, wrap-around display case and budtenders serving other customers on all sides. I've been listening in, absorbing what I can as I see them bringing out containers of pot and talking about the various attributes.

"What are my choices for edibles?" I ask. Last time I had an "edible" was when we made brownies in high school. We probably ate too much 'cause we were wrecked. In the display case separating Carl and me are a variety of chocolate bars, baked goods, gummies, other chewables, and who knows what else. I'm like a kid in a candy shop, at least an adult in a marijuana candy shop.

Carl pulls out a variety of chocolate bars, dark chocolate, bars with nuts, milk chocolate...

"The dark chocolate looks good. How much should I eat at once?" I ask.

"Well," he starts, "I'd begin with two squares and see how that feels."

"How much do you eat?" I wonder aloud.

"I eat a whole bar."

My eyes must have popped because he blurts out, "I have a high tolerance."

He's also a big dude. "Tell me about the bud," I ask.

Carl gives me a quick lesson about the differences between sativa

BIKING, LESSONS, BLESSINGS AND BEER

and indica. In a nutshell, the indica is for relaxation and calming, while the sativa is for uplift and energy. Carl also tells me that today's customer appreciation day which means 10 percent off everything, but I'm only here for a sampling, not a bulk order. I buy an indica chocolate bar, a vial of bud, and head out.

Departing Gresham, Steve and I are soon on bike lane highways. Portland's got three 350 miles of bike paths, bike lanes, and greenways complete with their own bike traffic signals. We share the routes with racers, commuters, kids, walkers, joggers, dogs, and homeless folks pushing shopping carts. Our destination for the night is western Portland at the home of Steve's college friend Warren, his wife Sharon, and their two daughters. We arrive early in the evening and are wined and dined with a delicious dinner, local beer and fine company.

July 29, 2017

Portland, Oregon

Today marks the end of another phase of the journey. Steve's gonna fly home from Portland and I'll stay with Emily, a former student whom I taught over a quarter of a century ago. After saying goodbye to my brother and friends, I cycle through this biker-friendly city to Emily's in northeast Portland. We catch up, have coffee, and I set my stuff in a small guest house out back. Portland's big and Emily's not a big biker, so we head downtown in her car where we walk along the riverfront, encounter a mermaid parade, eat burritos from a food cart, and spend hours at Powell's Books, the best bookstore ever. With a kind and generous host like Emily and my bike safely in her house, I'm an extremely grateful tourist.

In Portland with Emily

On the road back to Emily's we house pass a pot fair. Why not? When in Portland... It's in an exposition hall with vendors from a variety of growers, no samples, but swag. I'm given a "Hot Box Growers" t-shirt, finding out later from my daughter that hot boxing is "the practice of smoking marijuana in an enclosed space (e.g., a car or a small room) in order to maximize the narcotic effect," and give away the t-shirt to a much younger friend. There's a large band jamming, rich chocolate sans marijuana, and a party-like atmosphere. Portland. Afterwards, Emily and I go out to dinner and ice cream and call it a night.

July 30, 2017
Portland to Corvallis, Oregon – 104 miles

Sunday morning, I've had a great time with Emily and in Portland, and I have no specific destination, only south and west towards the California coast. With the forecast predicting a heat wave with temperatures over 100 degrees, I'm extremely glad to be heading to the cooler Pacific coast.

Southward bound, I toodle with a breeze at my back, and once out of the Portland area, the roads are spectacular with ample fine food stops. Riding in the Willamette Valley is reminiscent of Vermont scenery and biking conditions: fields, trees, gentle hills, good pavement, and shoulders. It's the sweetest riding since Montana: green, tranquil, and the land is comforting.

My first food stop is a wild blackberry patch on the side of the road. So many ripe ones to choose from and I eat a bunch. Next stop is Jones Farm Produce stand. The heck with fruit; they sell Umpqua ice cream. I don't care that it's morning. I'm an adult and a large dish of espresso chocolate chip is perfect at 10:30 a.m. As I'm eating my sweet, frozen breakfast outside, a biker comes over. Laurie's a transplanted Alaskan grandma who moved here to be close to her grandkids. She's prepping for an upcoming Oregon tour and we ride south together.

We stop at REI where I buy a tube and then ride to her home near Salem where she treats me to a lunch of brie and a baguette. After lunch I figure I may as well check out Salem. I have a Warm Showers in Corvallis tonight and plenty of time, so I bike around Riverfront City Park, the capitol, and stop for a coffee and pastry on a pleasant, quiet Sunday in Oregon's capital.

About an hour south of Salem I see a sign advertising a winery. The building's visible from the road; what the heck, might as well take a short detour. I park, head into the building, and say hi to the sommelier who's behind an ornate bar and with a customer. They have bins of fruit, so I buy apricots, peaches, and plums, and as I check out, the sommelier and I talk. When he hears what I'm doing, he insists I try the wines without charge. He doesn't have to twist my arm. Very tasty and soon I'm gliding along Route 99 with a slight buzz.

It's simply a gorgeous day, the ride is smooth, and as always,

BIKING, LESSONS, BLESSINGS AND BEER

heating up by mid-afternoon. As has been the story of this trip, all good things must come to an end. Twenty miles north of Corvallis my derailleur cable breaks again. That's bad. But the road has no serious hills. That's good. It's hot and I still have a ways to go in two gears. That's bad. Corvallis is home to Oregon State University and lots of bike shops. That's good. Worst case scenario, I'll be spending time in Corvallis tomorrow waiting for the bike shops to open and have my cable replaced.

A few hours later I make it to Corvallis a hot, sweaty mess. I'm challenged to find Lori and Mike's house on a cul-de-sac and eventually do. As Lori warmly receives me, I tell her of my equipment failure and ask her to recommend a bike shop. Better yet, she tells me, her husband Mike is an avid biker and engineer who loves working on bikes. Of course.

Mike arrives home soon, and we eat a delicious dinner in their backyard along with a tasty local brew. Lori and Mike are kind, bright, and traveling folks with two sons, one an engineer and one very much like my son Jake, adventurous and eager to change the world.

After dinner, while holding a flashlight in his teeth, Mike spends an hour replacing my derailleur cable and fixing the other, trying to make them perfect. All I can do is watch. I will indeed be getting out of Corvallis in the morning. I head to the enclosed porch that serves as my bedroom.

July 31, 2017

Corvallis to Florence, Oregon – 111 miles

I eat breakfast with Mike and Lori and feel unsettled. In all likelihood, today will be even more unusual than every other day. For the thousands of miles I've bicycled, almost without fail, I've moved westwardly. As I've clicked off 100 or so miles each day across our vast country, I've known I have a long way to go. Either consciously or unconsciously, I don't look at a U.S. map or even state maps very often, instead using only Adventure Cycling's sectional maps. Crossing the Mississippi River was a gateway to the West, reaching new state signs are welcome markers, going over the Rockies and the Continental Divide (a number of times mind you) all meant I was making my way across the continent. While packing up from Mike and Lori's, I realize that barring a serious mishap, this very afternoon I'll reach the Pacific Ocean, and I'm not sure how I feel about this milestone.

After saying goodbye and thanking Lori and Mike for all they provided me, I take a quick jaunt through Oregon State's campus and then ride west. Outside Corvallis I climb for most of 2 hours until I reach Alsea and take a break at Johnny Boy's Mercantile. Johnny Boy's is Alsea's version of Dan and Whit's, the store in my town whose

BIKING, LESSONS, BLESSINGS AND BEER

regionally famous motto proclaims: "If we don't have it, you don't need it." A traveler aptly described Johnny Boy's, "Where else can I score a bottle of hooch, coveralls made by inmates, a slingshot, ice cream sandwiches, assorted hardware, and fishing tackle, complete with advice on what's biting today?"

Named after a tribe who lived near the coast, Alsea was booming through the 1980s when environmental restrictions curbed harvests of federal timber. I imagine the spotted owl debate must have been raging here. Now it's a community of only 200 residents who mostly commute and a stopping point for those on their way to the coast like me.

I buy a muffin and eat it on the porch where I'm joined by Joe, a guy who grew up here, left, and came back. He seems to be my age, but after a life of smoking and who knows what else, looks and acts a lot feebler. He's friendly enough and wants to talk. I listen for a while, but I'm eager to get to the coast, so in a bit I bid Joe adieu.

Earlier this morning Mike recommended I take a cutoff that will put me on a more scenic and less-traveled route than Highway 34, albeit longer. I've got plenty of time so I'm game. As I start down the rural cut-off, I grow reflective, and I might add, sentimental, thinking about how close I am to arriving at the Pacific. It proves to be too early for that. Mike's detour takes me through wooded, unnamed roads. Highway 34 is remote, but this is forested backcountry. I have no cell phone service and no map. Mike made the route sound straightforward. Although the woods I ride through are picturesque, the terrain varied, and the traffic-free roads are in good shape, I'm not enjoying them as much as I ordinarily would. I'm unsettled.

After an hour and a half of shaded, up and down riding, I have my doubts. Am I on the right track? I know the Pacific Ocean is close, and I'll be disappointed if I don't get there today. It's still hard not to have expectations. Have faith, I tell myself. Mike's straight as an arrow and there haven't been any significant roads to turn on to and get lost. I soldier on and hope that I'm going the right way.

After what seems like forever, but is less than 2 hours, I'm back on Route 34, 15 miles west of Alsea. The road now has more cars and no more shoulder. By my count I have 20 miles to go. At some point in the very near future I'll spot the Pacific Ocean. For the first time in seven weeks and 4,000 miles of bicycling, I'm overcome by strange emotions. Tears well up. With every turn of the pedal, I'm that much closer to having crossed this country on my bicycle. It's no longer an abstraction. The thousands of miles in between the coasts, the states I had never before passed through, the ups and downs on my bicycle and in my mind, the people I have met, lessons I have learned, beer I have drunk, blessing bestowed on me are all winding down.

Emotions are roiling inside me, yet when I reach the sign welcoming me to Waldport, Oregon, I still can't see the ocean. I

BIKING, LESSONS, BLESSINGS AND BEER

continue downhill until I'm stopped at a traffic light at the intersection with Route 101, the coastal highway. On the other side of the road I see the Pacific Ocean. I cross to a nearly empty beach parking lot, lock my bike against a post, take off my shoes and walk down to the sand. As I put my feet into the frigid water, I start crying, then sobbing. Soon I'm full on bawling. A couple standing nearby, watching me, must be wondering what's going on with this guy? I blubber, "I just biked across the country." I'm overwhelmed. I had no idea I would feel this way. It isn't as if the Pacific Ocean was a goal and yet, as I stand in the sand, I'm overcome with emotions. I ask the couple to take my picture. I wish I had someone to share this with, my family especially. I call Jeannie. She answers and I can't get the words out, just sobs. "What's wrong?" she asks. I manage to eke out, "I did it!"

YES, XC. Feet in the Pacific.

After seven weeks I'll no longer point my front tire west. I pedaled out of my garage in Norwich, Vermont on June 8th. Today is July 31st. My front wheel has been oriented west for almost all of that time except for short jaunts south and north, the six days of pannier-free pleasure riding, and three days not on the bicycle at all. Forty-seven days biking west and now I'm standing at the Pacific Ocean. What now? There is no more Westward Ho.

I feel disoriented. From here on I'll be cruising south with an almost non-stop, can't-miss landmark on my right. Instead of facing headwinds, there'll be tailwinds coming from the north. I left home with a vague destination, but it certainly wasn't Waldport, Oregon nor the Pacific Ocean. Sacramento made sense as a place to end, now I'm not sure. I can continue biking as long as I want, and I'll make it to the Bar Mitzvah in time. This afternoon I make it as far as Florence, find a cheap motel on Route 101 but by the time I'm showered, it's dark and too far to walk to Old Town, so it's a trip to the grocery store and a night in the motel for me.

BIKING, LESSONS, BLESSINGS AND BEER

August 1, 2017

Florence to Port Orford, Oregon – 102 miles

I share Highway 101 with too many tourists, never enough slices of Redwood Forest, and frequent views of sand dunes and the breathtaking coastline. It's funny. The more tourists and people around, the more isolated I feel. The scenery is spectacular and the biking quite good considering the amount of people and vehicles, but I don't make connections. I enjoy ice cream in Newport and sit with a biking couple from Madrid. They started on the Mexican border but took a flight to Oregon to avoid the daunting headwinds. I meet a few guys from Great Britain and a couple from Germany, also on bikes.

Unfortunately, there won't be any Warm Showers until I get to California. In the afternoon I bypass a few state parks along 101 since I plan to camp in Port Orford. I arrive early evening and bike up a very long, very steep hill to Port Orford Heads State Park. There are stunning views, trails, a lifeboat museum and... no camping. Amazing. How did I not see that on the map? Another lesson that is taking too long to learn—pay attention map details, chucklehead. I bike back down the hill and find an old motel right across the street from Battle Rock Wayside Park, a picturesque coastal spot memorializing a skirmish between natives and settlers in 1851.

California

August 2, 2017

Port Orford, Oregon to Crescent City, California – 82 miles

The mind is an amazing thing. My healthy body has been integral to this trip's success. However, I attribute what's been transpiring in my head and how it regulates emotion and attitude as the true key to making this experience what it's been. In terms of geography, crossing the California state line late this afternoon is just another turn of the wheels. Emotionally it's much more than a new welcome sign or my 14th and final U.S. state. I still have almost 400 miles to Sacramento, but I'm in California and there will be no more new states. California was my destination and now

BIKING, LESSONS, BLESSINGS AND BEER

I'm here.

Since reaching the Pacific, I've been riding rolling hills with spectacular vistas and a gentle tailwind. It's not as if a weight has been lifted from me since not once during this trip did I feel a burden. It's never been, "Dang, I have to ride today." I've enjoyed getting on my bicycle and riding every single day, although certainly not every moment. Now everything from here on feels like icing on the cake. My flexible 100-mile-a-day goal is a thing of the past. I continue to ride as much as I want, but this means fewer miles. I no longer listen to the Sirens. I break longer and more frequently. And I plan my days to enjoy as many Warm Showers as I can.

I'm tired, physically and mentally. While I don't think this is new, I've ignored it to propel myself westward at a good clip. I use a lot of energy interacting with strangers, moving every day, staying in a new place each night, and absorbing so much stimulation. Maybe I've just held the tired at bay.

Immediately after entering California, I see a couple hitchhiking on the other side of the road. I remember my younger days hitching and vagabounding in the Golden State, although not as far north as I am now. I pedal over and learn they're from Michigan and are heading to Oregon seeking a new life. I listen to them describe their dreams that seem fantastical—communal living, travel, and intermittent work. He asks if I have a lighter. I loan it to him and he tells me he's been looking forward to smoking some of the weed he's been carrying. She's pregnant and doesn't partake. I do. I give them a few energy bars and hope they find what they seek.

Hitchin' Michigander hippies

Later I pass through the town of Fort Dick and then to my left is an enormous, fenced complex extending for what seems likes miles. Not only aren't there any welcome signs, there are no signs at all. When I see the guard towers, I know I'm outside Pelican Bay State Prison. Spanning 250 acres and holding over 2,000 inmates plus staff, it has three times more people than the town I just rode through. The prison's primary purpose is to house the "worst of the worst." Forty percent of Pelican Bay's inmates are serving life sentences and all have histories of violence at other California prisons. Prisoners in two of the cell blocks are kept in solitary confinement 22 hours a day, seven days a week, year after year. Talk about contrasts. I'm as free as can be, coming and going when and where I want. Separated from me by this fence are thousands of my fellow citizens, some of the most restricted people on earth.

Late in the afternoon, I arrive at the home of my first California Warm Showers host, Rob. He bike-toured in his younger days and his son has just begun the new crown jewel of American touring: biking from Alaska to the southern tip of Argentina. I can only vaguely imagine what this could be like.

Outdoor luxury

Rob's place is situated in a suburbanesque neighborhood and he's got quite the compound. There are gardens and fruit trees, some green houses, pot plants, outbuildings, and my "room."

Rob tells me that he has plans for more creative and sustainable living on this land, but the crown jewel of his domain are two acres of old growth redwoods. Unbelievable, one's own redwood grove, a Sequoian oasis, even if it is in the midst of a neighborhood. It's the reason he bought the place. I take a few walks through the stand during the afternoon, evening, and morning. Rob and I enjoy a satisfying bottle of Northern California "Lost Coast" beer and then we dine with his wife. As night falls, I head to my cozy shelter to read before sleeping and heading out the next morning.

Rob and his redwoods

BIKING, LESSONS, BLESSINGS AND BEER

August 3, 2017

Crescent City to Trinidad, California – 71 miles

My distance and pace have become, dare I say, relaxed. I'm taking longer and more frequent breaks. There are many beautiful sights: majestic redwoods, startling rock formations, beaches, and harbors. I'm feasting on chill riding, literally and figuratively, and generous hospitality. I ride in morning mist, under afternoon blue skies, through gigantic trees, past colorful lagoons, and without wind pushing against me. Life is good.

I'm psyched for another Warm Showers tonight, likely my last one. Evelyn and Wallace are welcoming, spiritual and bright souls, a bit older than me. Their home is close to highways and byways, yet they've created the oasis filled with gardens and lots of chickens. I camp in the yard with the birds. Evelyn, Wallace, and I have stimulating conversations about Humboldt County, their lives, their kids, philosophy, and they treat me to a delicious dinner, an Anchor Brewing Company beer, and a warm shower. I'm taken with a quote on Wallace and Evelyn's fridge by Mary Anne Radmacher.

Live with intention, walk to the edge, listen hard, practice wellness, play with abandon, laugh, choose with no regret, continue to learn, appreciate your friends, do what you love, live as if this is all there is.

Evelyn and Wallace suggest that I sleep in my tent as the dew that falls overnight is drenching. They weren't kidding. When I wake up my tent and gear are soaked.

August 4, 2017
Trinidad to Scotia, California – 60 miles

The end is near. I'm meeting Hannah sometime late this afternoon after she gets out of work. Riding to Sacramento has zero allure. Not only does the prospect of biking inland to Sacramento with its 100-degree-plus temperatures sound miserable, my daughter wants to escape the heat of the city. She'll meet me wherever I'll be this evening. As we communicate during the day, we decide upon Scotia. She picked Humboldt Redwoods State Park for us to camp this weekend.

I cross a narrow part of Arcata Bay and enter Eureka. I look for a "Eureka, You Found It!" welcome sign, but find none. I visit quaint Old Town, sit by the water, stop in a bagel cafe. For the first time on this trip I feel like I'm on vacation. Interesting, isn't it? Technically I've been "on vacation" for almost two months, if vacation means not

BIKING, LESSONS, BLESSINGS AND BEER

working. Yet as goal-focused as I've been, even when chilling, I've been on a mission. Like my layovers in Columbus, Iowa City, Missoula, and Fort Collins, today I truly feel like a tourist now moseying about on my own.

On the road I see several billboards encouraging me, yes me specifically, to "Visit Eel River Brewing." Since I'm going that way, I figure why not. I had such a good time at New Belgium Brewery, maybe I can relive the joy. When I get to Fortuna, I walk into Eel River Brewing and ask the hostess where the brewery is. Wrong place, this is only a brew pub. Their brewery is further south in Scotia. Later.

Mid-afternoon I get to Scotia, and using Google Maps, try to find Eel River Brewing. The maps take me behind an old, wooden, industrial-like building complex next to the railroad tracks. I bike on the pothole-filled dirt road and can't find any signs for Eel River Brewing. I ride back to the main street from where I came. Google Maps instructs me to head back to the industrial site where I just was. I listen, cross the tracks, and wipe out in the mud. I scan the back of the building—no signs welcoming me to Eel River Brewing Company. I pedal to the paved road again and still Google Maps are telling me to turn back. There's a certain poetic justice to this, getting lost within a quarter mile of where I will finish my summer's long trek, listening to Google Maps. The third time I return to the rear of the buildings, I go up to each door. When I get to the fourth entrance, I see a small Eel River Brewing Company sign above the door. It's no New Belgium. There are no welcome signs and surely no tours. I go in anyway. It's been a quest to find it and now that I'm successful, I have to drink from the holy grail.

I walk in and up several stairs. Seeing an office to my left, I enter and tell the two women working here who I am and why I'm here. They're friendly but tell me that they don't get visitors; this is a brewery not a tourist attraction. One of the women says she'll see if the brewmaster is here. She heads out, returns in a few minutes and tells me that he's not. He worked last night but she'll show me around. Eel River's a small operation and it's cool walking amidst a working brewery with kegs, mashers, fermenters, bags of grain, water on the floor, cases of beer, and even if there are no sampling stations, I'm grateful. I thank my host for the experience and her kindness.

After the "tour" I have time before Hannah arrives. I unpack my wet tent and rain fly, lay them out in front of the general store in Scotia to dry, and I sit. I'm done. My cross-country adventure is over. There are no finish lines, crowds cheering, ribbons, or medals. I lock my bike to a post and that's it. No one around knows or cares.

BIKING, LESSONS, BLESSINGS AND BEER

Eel River Brewery

Hannah arrives in an hour and it is so sweet to see her. I'm elated to be with my daughter and to realize that the ride truly is over. My bike has been my most steady companion for 56 days. Now I'll be with my family. It'll take time for it all to sink in.

Hank and I buy food and beer, Eel River IPA of course, for our camping trip in the Humboldt Redwoods. As Hannah and I start to drive out of Scotia, I remember that I left my tent outside the store to dry. My tent, the replacement for the inadequate bivy, the structure that sheltered me from rain and storms, my refuge from biting insects, and my security blanket. We turn back. When we get to the store the tent's not where I left it. Gone. You've got to be kidding. I get out of the car, look around, and spot a woman walking away from the store with the tent under her arm. I catch up to her and say,

"That's my tent."

"Oh, I thought someone had left it for the taking," she tells me.

What timing.

It's less likely that someone will take your tent if it is upright and assembled.

In Humboldt with Hannah

* * *

After a superb weekend biking, hiking, and camping in the redwoods, it's onto Sacramento and Jeannie's arrival. The three of us head to the Tetons and Yellowstone, but this time the miles fly by from the seat of a car. Through a spotting scope we definitely see one grizzly laying on a kill. I also see lots more confirmed grizzlies and wolves at the Grizzly and Wolf Discovery Center in West Yellowstone.

BIKING, LESSONS, BLESSINGS AND BEER

When we visit the Lamar Valley there are bison galore. We hike among them and marvel at their girth and magnificence. I do lots of hiking and some running, finally using my legs for something other than pedaling. I also have company, my wife and daughter. What a way to wrap up my travels.

But before I return East, there is the bar mitzvah. Noah leads, lectures, and recites magnificently. I spend time with my cousin Lori and catch up with Susie from Cleveland. With lots of family are around, it's a gratifying end to the summer.

Epilogue

August 22, 2017

Bradford and Norwich, Vermont

This morning, my first back home, I jump whole hog into my new job, head of school for adolescent boys with complex, developmental trauma. It was not a role I planned to assume but agreed when I was asked last May. Classes begin in a few days and the staff, especially me, has a lot to prepare. Almost all of our kids are state-placed, adjudicated, couldn't handle alternative schools, living with foster parents or grandparents. Most have no permanency plan; that is, they will not return to a family. Most have been horribly abused and/or neglected. For nearly all of these young gents we are their last chance before incarceration.

At school we make substantial progress throughout the year. We create safety and routines from an institution that had existed in chaos. For me, life's day to day regularity is a hard adjustment, much more difficult than I anticipated. For almost two months all I had to think about was following a route across the country. I woke, ate, stopped, and talked when I wanted. No more. I have a fixed schedule and countless obligations to others. I know it sounds selfish, but it was unbelievably liberating.

In spite of the difficult transition back to a typical life, bicycling cross-country was momentous and extremely gratifying. I imagine the voyage was similar to a spiritual retreat. I had countless hours to contemplate, live in the moment, reflect, and dream. I was also able to know so many strangers and see so much of our land. The adventure makes helps me appreciate what I have. I've known many people my age who continue to do what they always did, work where they always have, some are befallen by tragedy and many never do what they longed to do. While it's true that one never knows what tomorrow will bring at any age, as one grows older there are fewer tomorrows.

How do I balance security, no matter how impermanent, and preparing for the future with my need for risk, novelty, and growth?

Can I find challenge and satisfaction wherever I am, even at home? That's what I'm attempting, working as a teacher instead of as a principal and doing some gentleman farming and homesteading activities, things I've pondered for decades. We have an absolutely gorgeous home and land. I'm happy on days when I don't have to leave my property or neighborhood. I hope being a steward of this land and nurturing living things will provide satisfaction and fulfillment.

www.ingramcontent.com/pod-product-compliance
Lightning Source LLC
Chambersburg PA
CBHW070301010526
44108CB00039B/1443